This book is dedicated to my wife "Baf" – who loves animals and always keeps the home fires burning in her unswerving devotion to the whole family.

# CONTENTS

# ENDORSEMENTS

*"Russ Constant has embarked on a life-changing adventure by delving into the foundations of our Christian faith and excavating gems of gold lying deep in the soil of Judaism. His painstaking research and ability to relate that research to a Gentile Christian context is worthy of our close attention and will enlighten our understanding of Scripture. The insights he has gained and synthesised into this book will greatly reward the reader and especially those of us who try to expound the meaning of Scripture for today."*

Mr Graham Poland, Pastor, Grosvenor Evangelical Church, Barnstaple, North Devon, UK.

*Dear Russ,*

*My first reaction was that this must be published. I was blessed by so much. I thought I would read a couple of pages a day and get back to you eventually. As it turned out I couldn't put it down — so many wonderful insights and, if I might say so, superbly put together and written.*

*I was particularly grateful for the Rabbi Thomson website. I came across him a few years back speaking at Max Lucado's church on the significance of the Lord's supper which blew my mind and I have been preaching on it ever since.*

*May God bless you as you continue to write.*

*Every blessing,*

*Dick*

Mr. Dick Chammings, Ex-school headmaster; Elder, Grosvenor Evangelical Church, UK

# JEWISH BREAD

# BREAD

*for*

# GENTILE

# BEGGARS

## (or...*The Jewish Jesus for Beginners*)

## R. V. CONSTANT

OlivePress
צהר זית

JEWISH BREAD *for* **GENTILE BEGGARS!**

ISBN: 978-1-941173-30-5

Published by
Olive Press Messianic and Christian Publisher
olivepresspublisher.com
olivepressbooks@gmail.com

Front cover design and artwork by
Ryan Isaac
www.ryanisaacart.co.uk
@ryanisaacart
ryanisaacart@gmail.com

NOTE: Having a British author and an American publisher, the choice was made to mainly use British grammar and spelling. For example: the British ending "-ise" vs American ending "-ize," etc., were used to keep the author's British voice. The punctuation, however, is more American than British.

# PREFACE

## How this book is organised

This book contains a number of investigations into various parts of Scripture with the intention of illuminating them from a Jewish perspective. I have limited these studies to the Gospels as they are generally the best known and familiar parts of the Bible so newcomers to the Jewish perspective will probably already have a "take" on the Scriptures which they can compare and contrast with what is being offered here. Since the chapters are "stand alone," they appear in no particular order other than length, making it easier for the reader to "dip in" to the shorter ones first before tackling the lengthier ones. But first...

## Something is missing

About 15 years ago, as far as the Bible was concerned, I had become bored. It seemed to me that the scriptures consisted of too many "bits" which often stood alone, disconnected from each other and therefore, while the "parts" were hard to understand at times, the "whole" also lacked a sense of overall coherence. Then someone handed me a video of a Jewish teacher who believed that Yeshua (the Hebrew name for Jesus) was the Messiah (the Christ). Dutifully, I watched it—in a neutral kind of way—and although not exactly "wowed', I did sense a spark of interest and like the man looking through the mist, I felt there was "something there" though I was not sure what exactly. Perhaps, I mused, investigating the Bible from a Jewish roots perspective might offer the brand new direction of travel I was seeking. But, I queried, surely this stuff isn't, well, "kosher', if you pardon the pun. After all, I didn't know any other evangelical believers who were into this "Jewish" thing…and isn't Judaism a different religion anyway?

## Searching for the "something"…

I then began searching Messianic Jewish websites cautiously—even suspiciously. What if I was being lured by wicked Jewish "sirens" onto the rocks of theological heresy in an attempt to rob me of my salvation by grace? After all, in the New Testament, didn't some Jews try telling new believers that they had to obey the Law of Moses to be saved? As I cautiously tiptoed through the teaching on these sites, I became aware of, what could be described in all honesty, as a latent, personal anti-Jewishness—vague background beliefs that God was not interested in the Jews anymore, that we Gentiles had replaced the Jewish people in His plan of salvation for the world, and thus, that the Old Testament, being the book of Judaism was inferior to the New; that it spoke of an angry God who, having attended anger management classes, had gotten over His attitude problem and had sent His son to show His new, more emotionally intelligent side.

## The "something" found…

And so I trawled through these websites like a family of meerkats I saw on TV once, who having chanced upon a snake were suspicious of what it might do but whose curiosity was so overwhelming that they just could not leave it alone! And as I did, I watched and waited for some theological toxin to strike, which would render this new direction of travel unacceptable, necessitating a rapid and sighing withdrawal to my original "slough of despond." However, no such event ever occurred and, to be honest, I have never looked back since.

When I consider my former suspicions about approaching the Bible from a Jewish perspective, I am struck by their sheer absurdity! After all, is it really so strange to study a book written exclusively by *Jews*, about a *Jewish* homeland which was visited by the *Jewish* Saviour who had *Jewish* disciples and who said that "...salvation is of the *Jews*', ... is it then, really so odd to approach our study of such a book from a *Jewish* perspective? Do we not favour sending our language students to the native country of that language, to be taught by a native speaker who is aware of the local sayings, traditions, and culture—and all the more so when that culture is set in a historical context dating back and spanning thousands of years?

## What went wrong...

Although this seems plain common sense, most of we Gentile believers spend our entire lives under the teaching of *Gentile* not *Jewish* Bible teachers—and this despite the fact that God even chose a *Jew*—Sha'ul (sometimes known as Paul)—to take the Gospel to the *Gentiles*. Please do not misunderstand me, I have learned much from Gentile teachers and have been glad of them. However, the apostle Paul pointed out that in God's "ecology," it is we *Gentiles* who are grafted into a *Jewish* olive tree (a symbol of Israel), despite our actual behaviour suggesting the opposite. We can sit in church for year after year and never hear a word about the Jewish festivals (which the Bible actually calls *God's* festivals), or how the customs and traditions of ancient Israel affect our interpretation of the words and deeds of Yeshua (Jesus).

Let's face it, this self-repositioning by Gentile believers is at best, a "helluva cheek," and at worst, makes us one of those the apostle Paul warned in the letter to the Romans as being guilty of Gentile arrogance. This, in turn has led to that most egregious of errors—the doctrine which asserts that the Gentile church has actually replaced the Jews and all of God's promises made to them have now been transferred to the Gentiles. This is known as REPLACEMENT THEOLOGY.

Originally of course, it was not so. The church was all Jewish at its inception but as the Gospel successfully spread across the Roman world, Gentile numerical superiority diluted the original Jewish ethnic identity out of the church. Leaders such as the Roman Emperor Constantine underwent a "technical" conversion to Christianity for political reasons and in 325 CE convened a meeting of bishops in what came to be known as *"The Council of Nicea."* Up to this point, the church's Jewish roots were still in evidence with Passover being celebrated and the seventh day of the week still being regarded as the Sabbath as God had commanded. By the time the council were finished, Constantine had replaced God's Sabbath with his own pagan *"venerable day of the sun (god)"* [1]...and the Passover with Easter,[2] a counterfeit substitute festival based on a pagan fertility goddess, a

1 "Sunday: Christian Usage," Wikipedia, https://en.wikipedia.org/wiki/Sunday#Christian_usage
2 "First Council of Nicea" and "Separation of Easter computation from Jewish calendar," Wikipedia, https://en.wikipedia.org/wiki/First_Council_of_Nicaea#Overview

11

rigorous and honest historical study of which will make your hair curl, despite the church's attempts to mask the fact with bunnies and chocolate eggs!

Our Bibles have also suffered as this overt or subconscious anti-Jewish culture has developed over time, not helped by the lack of Jews on the Bible translation committees. What follows is a few examples of this anti-Jewish bias:

## What a difference a comma can make!

It is remarkable how minute changes in punctuation can make such a huge difference and lead to a totally false impression. For instance, notice how different translations deal with Yeshua's warning about scribes in Luke 20:46-47:

KJV - *"Beware of the scribes, which..."*

RSV - *"Beware of the scribes, who like to go about in long robes..."*

NIV - As he taught, Jesus said, *"Watch out for the teachers of the law. They like to walk around in flowing robes and be greeted in the marketplaces..."*

Inserting that comma makes Yeshua's warning seem to apply to *every single Jewish scribe.* The NIV Bible translation even goes one step further by condemning every teacher of the law by using a full stop! Interestingly, not only does the Greek text *not* support this comma, but worse, by including *all* the scribes and teachers of the law, the translators have effectively slandered all the good ones along with the bad. This is a serious sin in Torah law and is effectively bearing *"false witness."* (It also makes God out to be a liar since Yeshua would be claiming that He opposes all Torah teachers, which is simply not true).

Now check out how Dr David Stern translates it in the *Complete Jewish Bible*...and see the difference!

CJB - As he taught them, he said, *"Watch out for the **kind of** Torah teachers who like to walk..."*

...surely, a simple but very significant improving adjustment to a definite anti-Jewish textual bias.

## The names of characters

A French friend of mine has a son called Guillaume (pronounced *Gee-om*). The equivalent name in English would be William, but I would never call him William since that is not his name. Such an Anglicisation would seem rude at best and racist at worst (especially since there is historical antipathy between the French and English). In fact, it might seem to him that I was trying to diminish, or deny his French identity by trying to make him sound English. And so this being the case, why have we replaced all the Bible's Jewish names with English ones? Is it not absurdly incongruous to come across the name *John* and *James* in the Bible's exclusively Jewish context? An examination of the Greek text where the name *James* is mentioned makes it clear that he actually had the Hebrew name *Jacob* (*Yaakov* in the Hebrew Old Testament— *Iakobos* in the Greek New Testament). So what happened? It appears that his name was translated as *James* to flatter *King* James, the patron of his eponymous translation, the *King James Version*. The name James has been accepted ever since.

But what about Paul? Some have been taught that Sha'ul (Saul of Tarsus) changed his Hebrew name to the

Greek name Paul following his acceptance of Yeshua as Messiah. This fits conveniently with the replacement theology viewpoint which claims that Paul ceased to be Jewish when he became a "Christian" and enables people to interpret Paul's teachings in terms of Christ having done away with "The Law." However, Dr David Stern, in his translation, *The Complete Jewish Bible*, notes that Saul would have had *two* names, as did many Jews living outside Israel (then as now). He had a *Greek* name for use in his Gentile home town, but he also had the *Hebrew* name which he received at his circumcision. Sha'ul never ceased to be a Jew—he merely became a properly *fulfilled* one in Yeshua. Paul did not see himself as a Christian; rather, he was a fully physical and (following his acceptance of Yeshua), fully *spiritual* Jew.

Probably the best (or worst) case of missed opportunity is the conversion of "*Yeshua*" to the vacuously de-contextualised "*Jesus*" (via "*Iosus*" in Greek), which conceals His Jewish identity and strips the meaning of so many Scriptures, such as Matthew 1:21 and Luke 2:30. Since the Name, Yeshua, essentially means "*salvation*," just imagine the effect on our Bible reading if the word Yeshua was used, not just as Jesus' real name but also instead of the word "*salvation*"— just imagine all the connections we would see! And of course, a similar fate has befallen the Bible's place names. When we consider the trouble the translators have taken to expunge the Jewishness from the Bible, we would be naïve not to consider that an alternative agenda was in some way, driving their decisions, all the more when all they had to do was, to coin a phrase, "leave well alone"!

## The Jews' opposition of Yeshua

As we read the Gospels, it could easily seem to us that the Jews were a continual nuisance to Yeshua to the point where we start to believe that Yeshua was attempting to start a new religion but was being opposed by marauding swarms of bigoted, legalistic Jews. The truth is though, as Dr David Stern points out in his *Jewish New Testament Commentary*, that Yeshua was opposed by the *Judeans*, meaning, the city sophisticates and ruling religious elite, as distinct from the common country people like Himself. Interestingly, Hebraic linguists inform us that the name *"Judas **Iscariot**"* originated from *"Yehuda ish kyriat"* —the Hebrew for *"Judas the **city man**"* —to distinguish him from *Galileeans* who were **countrymen**. As far as opposition to Yeshua is concerned, this rebalancing shifts the weight of opposition to a minority only. Again though, the subtle bias is there.

## The phrase: "The Law"

This is a most unfortunate translation used in our Bibles. This phrase is used to refer to the Mosaic Law as given to the Hebrew nation by God via Moshe (Moses). However, although laws were of course a constituent part of what God gave, a much better translation would be *"instruction"* or *"teaching,"* and is referred to "in the round" as the "Torah." Using the phrase "The Law" tends to limit the scope of what God gave at Mt. Sinai, implying that it was only a set of legalistic and draconian rules. Our tendency to spend a disproportionate amount of time in the New Testament

15

(where the Torah can appear negatively associated with some Jews who were keen to use it cynically as a trap with which to catch Yeshua out) tends to further exacerbate the anti-Jewish bias.

This perspective on the Law of Moshe has led to us setting up a false dichotomy, forcing us to choose between salvation through works (the Law) and salvation by faith (through Messiah Yeshua). I say "false" because the Bible does not, in fact, present The Law as a means of salvation. It was the Hebrews' exodus from Egypt, which the Bible correlates with their deliverance/ salvation—and what is more, they escaped Egypt (a symbol of sin) by faith as stated in Hebrews 11. Law was given later as teachings on how to live as a people *once* they had been redeemed! Moreover, Rahab, the Gentile, was justified by *faith*—not for obeying the Law. All the Jewish "heroes" cited in Hebrews 11— Gideon, Barak, Samson, Jephthah, David and Samuel —*all* of them were commended and justified *by faith*—not by works or for observing the Torah.

In fact, even the sacrifices required by The Law and presented by Hebrews were only truly viewed by God as efficacious if they were offered with faith. Rabbi Daniel Thomson (of *Jewisheyes*) tells the fictitious story of two men presenting identical male lambs for slaughter at Pesach (Passover). One of them comments: *"Oh isn't it marvellous how God delivered us from the bondage of Egyptian slavery and protected us from the same judgment which befell the Egyptians?!"* ...While the other replies, *"You don't mean to say you believe all that hogwash? I just go along with it to keep everyone happy—you know, it's just a tradition!"* The

16

Rabbi asks the question, *"Which one went away justified?"*
According to Hebrews 11, it can only be the former since
when Abel presented his sacrifice, he mixed it with faith and
*"...by faith...was commended as righteous, when God spoke
well of his offerings."*

In short, Torah observance was never meant to be a
means of salvation; the false choice between law and grace
is a tradition of man—not God!

There are other anti-Jewish prejudices in some of
our translations but I have included just a few to get you
thinking about this problem. As the Jewish Hebrew teacher
and poet, Haim Nachman Bialik, once said,*"Reading the
Scriptures in a translation (from Hebrew) is like kissing your
bride through a handkerchief."* [3] Strive to get as close to the
original as you can!

## What to do after this book

If, after reading this book, you would like to find out more
or follow a systematic study plan of some kind, I would like
to strongly recommend the following three websites. Each
is excellent in it's own way and satisfies the most important
criterion for acceptability as far as I am concerned, which is
that salvation is by faith in Messiah Yeshua (Christ Jesus)
alone and not by works. This needs to be made clear at the
outset as, like me, you may be concerned that these sites
advocate that following The Law of Moses is the way to be
saved. This is a correct definition of the term "legalism" and
is rejected by all these sites:

---

3 Haim Nachman Bialik, Jewish Poet, 1873-1934, famous quote by him.

| Website | My comments | Their attitude to The Torah |
|---------|-------------|------------------------------|
| Ariel Ministries | Excellent, solid, lots of materials some of which are free. The founder, Arnold Fruchtenbaum wrote the best, most systematic exposition on the "end times" I have ever read called *Footsteps of the Messiah* (see Bibliography.). | Ariel are very straightforward. They are "dispensational" meaning they believe "The Law of Moses" was in force for a period of time which ended when the Messiah died. |
| Torah class.com | Excellent, thought-provoking intellectually but in a way which can be understood. Particularly good at emphasising the Hebrew "God patterns" which demonstrate how God "organizes" the past, present, and future. The free audio downloads can be followed on the dictation script provided. | Torahclass are not so sure about what has happened to the Torah as Ariel ministries are. They believe that the Torah still has relevance today but "how" exactly is debated at various points. |
| Jewish eyes.org | A remarkable insight into the Scriptures from a Jew who skilfully uses Jewish writings to reach precision interpretations of Scriptures. His insights will revolutionize your thinking, and in some cases, even reverse it! | Rabbi Daniel Thomson is the "real deal"! He believes that the Torah is alive and well and greatly benefits the life of the believer in Yeshua. You will be amazed at how close your opinion will shift in favour of this position—if—you remain open-minded and are prepared to let any prejudices go! Even if you do not adopt his position, it is fascinating to hear or read his insights. |

In retrospect, I suddenly realised that perhaps I did not happen upon these websites by accident but rather, was guided to them over a period of years beginning with *Ariel Ministries*, then *TorahClass* and finally *Jewisheyes*. I now believe that I was being taken on a 3-stage journey which had to be gradual in the sense that I needed exposure to increasingly "strong meat," (as Sha'ul—Paul—put it) in a gentle and progressive way. This is not to imply that *Ariel* are by any means inferior to *Jewisheyes*, but rather that *Ariel*'s position on The Law of Moses is much closer to the average Evangelical's view which makes them an ideal choice for the Christian who is curious about the Jewish roots movement. Speaking personally, I entertained a number of immature and unhelpful prejudices which would have caused me to reject the ministry of *Jewisheyes* outright due to its positive stance on The Torah. I would also have struggled with Rabbi Daniel Thomson's use of extra-Biblical sources such as the Talmud—a huge Jewish hyper-text commentary which, although not Scripture, is actually immensely helpful in understanding the social and cultural context within which Yeshua spoke and acted.

As a result, I now realise just how much Yeshua *did* use those well known stories, legends, and existing parables which were already very familiar to His Jewish audiences as a way of connecting with them, whereas, we Gentiles tend to erroneously think that everything Yeshua said was separate from His Jewish culture. One of the negative consequences of this include the common belief amongst many Jews that Jesus is not for them since He is the God of the Gentiles, supported by the (untrue) tradition that He spoke against the Torah.

19

## What you can expect...

The object of this book is to whet your appetite for a change of approach to your Bible reading and study towards studying Scripture from a Jewish roots perspective. As you do this, you may (and hopefully will) benefit in these ways:

- Puzzling Scriptures will suddenly make sense

- You will be able to "see through" certain ungodly beliefs you may hold (and not even be aware of) regarding the Jewish people, the corollary of which will be a love and concern for God's chosen people which you may not have had previously.

- The Bible will seem more connected because you are beginning to "see" it through the right "glasses," or if you like, the proper (Jewish) lens.

- Yeshua and Biblical events in general will begin to take on a 3-dimensional quality, like contours suddenly rising upward from a flat map. Colour, detail, texture and relief will begin to fill in this "Scripture mapscape" and the Bible will progressively spring to life.

- The sayings of Yeshua which seem to come "out of the blue" and appear unrelated to the immediate context will begin to make sense, giving the text greater cohesion and overall sense.

- When God effectively "invented" Israel by promising Abraham that he would become a great nation, He extended the promise by adding in Genesis 12 — *I will* (also) *bless those who bless you.* In aligning yourself with the Jewish people, you will be "activating" this, one of God's earliest and broadest promises for anyone and everyone.

- You will start looking for and noticing the "God patterns" which will enhance the overall cohesion and unity of the Scriptures.

- You will have the comfort and satisfaction of knowing that you are participating in a world-wide revival of interest in the Jewish roots of Christianity which is undoubtedly a work of God in preparation for His end-time plans, central to which will be Israel and the Jewish people. As Sha'ul (Paul) told us ...*and all Israel will be saved.*

- ...As Yeshua said, *"Come and see."*

May God bless you in this new and life-changing undertaking!

21

*The lamp of the body is the eye.*

*If your eye is good,*

*your whole body is full of light;*

*but if your eye is evil*

*your whole body is full of darkness...*

(Matthew 6:22)

# GOOD EYE—BAD EYE

> Quick Summary! There are occasions when Yeshua said things, which seem "out of the blue" and unrelated to the immediate context. However, by familiarising ourselves with: a) the Jewish cultural context and b) how and where similar phrases are used elsewhere in the Bible, these odd sounding passages do, in fact, make sense and are there to be understood.

## And now in more detail...

This text is a classic case where a lack of knowledge of Jewish sayings and idioms has so easily led us to false, "guesswork" interpretations. The standard interpretation used to assume this to be a cautionary warning to monitor what we let our eyes see, as it were, the "visual company" we keep, with television being a good contemporary example. Although a fair point in itself, this is not the primary meaning here. The phrase, *if your eye is good* is actually from the Jewish idiom *good eye* which means "being generous," while, *evil eye,* means "stingy and tight-fisted," which has nothing to do with evil looks or spells as some Bibles' footnotes suggest.

My own misunderstanding resulted from ignoring one of the golden rules of Scriptural interpretation, namely: CONTEXT is KING! In this particular case, taking into account what comes *before* and *after* this passage would have clinched the meaning on its own. If only commentators had looked honestly at the surrounding text then its subject would have been obvious as it comes sandwiched between two other texts **both focusing on money**. Look at the passage from Mattityahu (Matthew) this way:

| Reference | Scripture | Subject |
|---|---|---|
| v 21 | *For where your* **wealth** *is, there your heart will be also.* | Money |
| v 22-23 | *"Good eye"/ "Evil eye"* metaphor. | ? |
| v 24 | *You can't be a slave to both God and* **money**. | Money |

If only we approached Scripture with an understanding or at least awareness of both the immediate *and cultural* context, then many of our errors would be avoided. In the particular example above, the immediate context should have been a dead give away by itself, even assuming no cultural knowledge! Since the subject of the Scripture preceding the "good eye/evil eye" metaphor is money as is the verse following, then it follows that the intermediate verse is also very likely to also concern money as **the essential context has not changed**. Thus, we should not be surprised that the CJB (*The Complete Jewish Bible*) translates this passage as,

> So if you have a "good eye," (that is, you are **generous**) your whole body will be full of light; but

24

*if you have an "evil eye" (that is, you are **stingy**),
your whole body will be full of darkness."*

The main problem we have as readers of the Bible in the "here and now" is that Yeshua lived and spoke in the "there and then" so-to-speak. It is not always obvious when we are encountering a Jewish idiom since they are often presented through a common writing style known as *"parallelism'*. In our "good eye" example, we may think that the Greek will come to our assistance but this phrase makes no more sense when we do check the Greek out since, although Greek was widely understood, Hebrew remained the *cultural* language of the day.

It is interesting to note just how the church has added another nail in the coffin of the Bible's Jewishness by seeing the New Testament as Greek and the Old as Hebrew, and indeed, many scholars are now rejecting this false dichotomy. No—we need to allow the Bible to interpret itself, which means learning to think a little more like a Hebrew.

The Book of Proverbs is a good example of the use of parallelism. Proverbs often come in pairs of phrases which seem to be disconnected which explains why so many of us, as decontextualised readers, find them mystifying. For example, in the Hebrew, Proverbs 22:9 says:

*He who has a **good eye** shall be blessed;
For he gives his bread to the poor.*

Parallelism has been used here which means that a graphic or non-literal phrase has been used (the 1st line) followed by its explanation or *application* (the 2nd line). Some commentators suggest solving these idioms by approaching them as a question and answer thus:

1ˢᵗ line (Question): *Who is it that has a **"good eye"**?*

2ⁿᵈ line (Answer): *He who gives his bread to the poor.*

A further parallelism on the same theme is found in Deuteronomy 15:9:

> *Beware lest there be an evil thought in your heart, saying, "The seventh year, the year of release, is at hand," and your **eye be evil** against your brother and you give him nothing.*

Again, in the form of a question-answer...

1.  (Question): *Who is it that has an **"evil eye"**?*
2.  (Answer): *The one who gives his poor brother nothing.*

So between Proverbs 22 and Deuteronomy 15, it is clear what Yeshua would have meant by a "good eye" and an "evil eye" —generosity towards the poor. Rabbi Daniel Thomson of *Jewisheyes* also adds to this idea of a "good eye" filling your body with light because you *see* your poor brother's need, meaning you acknowledge it with action, compared with the body which is full of darkness because you are *blind* to what is in front of you and refuse to allow its "light" in to affect your internal will, since your observation is not accompanied by positive and responsive action. Therefore, if even your "light" is dark, then how dark must your entire body (your internal condition) be.

Having established the meaning of the "good eye" passage through an appreciation of Jewish idiom and parallelism, we should also be aware of an additional device used by Matthew designed to elevate the divine status of its contents. Matthew had a penchant for organizing his Gospel using *triplets*, or what modern writers might call, "the rule of three." Unfortunately, with Jews not having been exactly over-represented on Scripture translation committees, our Bibles are not set out in a way that is sensitive to Matthew's richly sophisticated literary forms, leaving us instead with the blunt instrument of verse and chapter breaks, the significance of which (as a human invention) is doubtful at times and serve only to create fracture lines across his intended structures. For instance, Matthew 8 and 9 contain nine miracles, which seem to have been organized into three groups of three, evidenced by the inclusion of pairs of questions like so:

*3 Miracles + 2 Questions,* followed by...

*3 Miracles + 2 Questions*, followed by...

*3 Miracles*

Paul Gaechter, in his book, *Literary Art in the Gospel of Matthew* points out that the number three represents "... *perfection, holiness and divinity"* [4] and the "good eye" passage is an example of this three-fold pattern—Matthew's way of encoding into the text, a "certificate" of divine endorsement. (E.W.Bullinger, in his book, *Number in Scripture*, supports this idea.[5])

This "good eye" passage teaches us that when Yeshua says something which seems to be out of context and unrelated to the text around it, the chances are, it is not that He has a "butterfly mind" but rather, it suggests that we simply lack

---

4 Paul Gaechter, *Literary Art in the Gospel of Matthew*, Katholisches Bibelwerk, 2013, https://chiasmusresources.org/title.

5 E.W.Bullinger, *Number in Scripture: Its Supernatural Design and Spiritual Significance,* Eyre & Spottiswoode (Bible Warehouse) Ltd, 1921, Alacrity Press, 2014, pp. 74-75, 77-78 .

the cultural knowledge to make sense of it. It has been said that humans would rather reach a *wrong* conclusion than *no conclusion* at all. The discomfort we feel when faced with two apparently contradictory truths is known as *cognitive dissonance*. Relating this to Scripture, this means that we have a tendency to react to our lack of understanding by saying to ourselves, "*I know this must make sense somehow, so I must **make it** make sense*"...if necessary by defaulting to the only knowledge we possess on the matter, however limited.

When this kind of situation arises, rather than resolving this discomfort by "forcing" upon a Scripture a best-guess interpretation from our own Gentile frame of reference, let us do the far more rewarding thing, let us turn to the Jewish sages and commentators—past and present—to enlighten us. And, as Scriptures begin to cohere with others, we will find the theme of a passage, "the picture on the jigsaw box," gradually emerging into something greater than the sum of its pieces.

*The people were amazed*

*at his teaching,*

*because he taught*

*them as one who had authority,*

*not as the teachers of the law.*

(Mark 1:22)

# AUTHORITY—JEWISH STYLE!

> **Quick Summary!** The Gospels tell us that Yeshua taught "with authority." We have our own understanding of what "authority" means but to the Jews of Yeshua's days, this meant something quite specific and unusual in the context of Rabbinic teachers.

## And now in more detail...

One of the characteristics of Yeshua's teaching which impressed, even amazed, His listeners was His *authority*. But what exactly did authority *mean* in the Jewish context of the day?

There are two common understandings in circulation. First, because of the *divine source* of His Words, Yeshua's Words carried with them natural weight and gravitas. This was definitely part of the meaning. In fact, in one circumstance in the Garden of Gethsemane, the power of His Words was so strong that those seeking His arrest actually drew back apparently under its sheer force. But that much effect seemed to be the exception, not the rule. The second understanding is that Yeshua spoke with an *authoritative manner*—a kind of stylised, confident, low, booming voice such as that used by American CNN newsreaders! This also could have been true since huge crowds seemed to have no trouble hearing Him. However, there remains another, more significant meaning.

To discover this other meaning, we need to turn to the ancient Jewish writings and determine how the Jewish sages and commentators gave weight to *their* points of view. Take a look at this example from an ancient source, of how a Jewish sage works towards making his point. He says...

> Did not Rabbi Itz'hak son of Joseph in the name of Rabbi Jo'hanan say: Rabbi R. Jehuda son of Roietz, the school of Shamai, Rabbi Simeon, and Rabbi Aqiba all hold that....[6]

...or putting it another way so we see the method more easily...

> Did not Joe, in the name of Mike say that Bill, Harry, and John all say that...

This somewhat convoluted way of communicating is the way that Jewish sages spoke and wrote. The idea was to *invoke* a number of other reputable sages or tutors who agreed with their point of view so as to lend more weight to their argument than would otherwise be the case if they simply quoted their own ideas in "a vacuum" so-to-speak. The point is, that a Rabbi did not generate *his own* authority but rather used the cumulative weight of a network of others

---

6 *Babylonian Talmud*, Order: Nezikin (Damages), Tractate Maccot (Makkot): Chapter 2, Gemara of Mishna II.

to support his argument. This was not seen as *copying* but rather as a demonstration of validity through *concensus*.

But the real point of quoting what previous rabbis have said is that in Hebrew understanding, the objective of a rabbi's disciple was to become a *replica*—a carbon copy of their tutor. Rabbi Daniel Thomson of *Jewisheyes* makes this point very well when he says that a disciple would, by close observation, copy exactly, every facet of their rabbi's behaviour—how they spoke, what they ate, even *how* they ate, etc, etc. To our modern, westernised way of thinking where individualism and self-expression are greatly esteemed, expending such great effort to reproduce our teacher's behaviours in minute detail seems completely anathema. But let us turn to what our own Jewish master says in Luke 6:40...

> *The student is not above the teacher, but **everyone who is fully trained will be like their teacher.***

Therefore, this explains why the Jewish writers invoked the names of previous rabbis because *they **wanted to be like** their tutor, (Rabbi so-and-so who was discipled by Rabbi so-and-so who was discipled by Rabbi so-and-so) since, like the "Russian doll" effect, to be like your Rabbi meant being like *his* tutor... who was like *his* tutor...and so on.

Therefore, since our key Scripture says that *He (Yeshua) had authority*, it is almost definite that Yeshua **did not** use this traditional method but His ability to silence His critics nonetheless was what amazed the crowd. By *not* using this method, Yeshua was strongly implying that **no-one** had taught Him which was yet another way of provoking the audience to ask the question in Matthew 13:54, *"Where did this man get this wisdom (authority)?"* It was this lack of reliance on others to support His arguments that the crowd considered **true authority**. This also explains the use by Yeshua of the phrase, *"You have heard it **said**, but **I say**…"* And once again, Yeshua skilfully and knowingly guides the central issue of His origins into the audience's field of view.

There is also a further "technique" which Jewish Rabbis used to indicate authority which is to be found liberally in the Gospels, and it is really quite obvious:

> *…he went up on a mountainside and **sat down*** (Matthew 5:1; 15:29 and John 6:3).

> *…Then he rolled up the scroll, gave it back to the attendant and **sat down*** (Luke 4:20).

> *…Then he **sat down** and taught the people from the boat* (Luke 5:3).

> *…and he **sat down** to teach them (John 8:1).*

It is clear from the above Scriptures that Yeshua always sat down to teach. (Curiously, we Gentiles stand to preach and it is the listeners who sit down). As to how this tradition came about, a clue is found in Exodus 18:13 where we read:

> *The next day **Moses took his seat** to serve as judge for the people, and they stood around him from morning till evening.*

Jethro, Moses' father-in-law then asked why Moses was managing the Israelite's problems, essentially, alone, and here's the answer in verse 15:

> *Moses answered him, "Because the people come to me to seek God's will. Whenever they have a dis-*

*pute, it is brought to me, and I decide between the parties and inform them of God's decrees and instructions."*

Since Moses "took his seat" to teach "God's decrees and judgments" then the thinking was that a Rabbi would also sit down to teach his listeners, sitting, so-to-speak, in Moses' seat. This is another good example of the esteem with which Moses was and is regarded since that tradition was still going strong 1400 years after the fact. It is clear from the Exodus reference that Moses' responsibility was to interpret the Law which God had given at Mt. Sinai and that meant authority—authority to define and explain exactly how these statutes may be applied both in personal and societal life. This is what Yeshua meant when he said in Matthew 23:2:

> *"The teachers of the law and the Pharisees **sit in Moses' seat**. So you must be careful to do everything they tell you. But do not do what they do, for they do not practice what they preach."*

Yeshua was saying that the Pharisees had the job of teaching the Laws of God and were therefore to be obeyed (as long as they *were* teaching God's Laws and not the traditions of men). Interestingly, there is a treatise written by a 14th century Jewish physician containing a Hebrew version (yes, take note: a *Hebrew* version) of this Scripture from Matthew's Gospel which has been translated by Nehemia Gordon, a Karaite Jewish scholar as follows:

> *"The Pharisees and sages sit upon the seat of Moses. Therefore, all that **he** (Moses) says to you, diligently do, but according to **their** reforms*

*(takanot) and **their** precedents (ma'asim) do not
do, because they talk but do not do."*[7]

This is illuminating as it shifts the focus on to the
listener doing all that *Moses* commanded, not the *Pharisees*.
It is interesting that even when a Jewish teacher is "sitting
down," they do so in reverential deference to Moshe (Moses),
further underlining the profound respect for that Patriarch.
A beautifully carved example of "Moses' seat" has been
discovered in the excavated synagogue of Chorazin—one of
the towns cursed by Yeshua. This is where the chief elder
would sit and the understanding is, that his word would be
final—fitting symbolism for believers to have in mind when
we read that Yeshua *sat down to teach.*

7 Nehemia Gordan, *The Hebrew Yeshua vs. the Greek Jesus,* Chapter 8
"Moses Seat," 3rd edition, Hilkiah Press, Atascosa, Texas, 2005, p. 47.

*After six days Jesus took Peter, James and John with him and led them up a high mountain, where they were all alone. There he was transfigured before them. His clothes became dazzling white, whiter than anyone in the world could bleach them. And there appeared before them Elijah and Moses, who were talking with Jesus.*

*Peter said to Jesus, "Rabbi, it is good for us to be here. Let us put up three shelters—one for you, one for Moses and one for Elijah." (He did not know what to say, they were so frightened.)* (Mark 9:2-6)

# Right Festival—Wrong order!

> **Quick Summary!** Although Peter did not know what to say in response to the awesome events to which they were privileged to witness, his desire to erect three shelters may in fact have made more sense than we think. It is likely that Peter's seemingly random offer was an instinctive abreaction which, although misplaced at the time, was in fact scripturally valid being rooted in one of the Jewish feasts.

## And now in more detail...

Before I began studying the Bible from a Jewish perspective, I assumed that Peter was simply babbling a lot of nonsense as a perfectly understandable reaction to the awesome and unexpected sight of Yeshua's spectacular transformation. However, we may be doing Peter something of a disservice.

[Before looking at Peter's comments, it is worth mentioning that Matthew and Mark indicate that this great event occurred *six* days after the previous happening while Luke says *eight* days. The solution to this apparent contradiction here is that Matthew and Mark (aimed primarily at Jews) used the Jewish system, numbering the days *between* two events, while Luke (aimed chiefly at Gentiles) used the Roman system counting the days on which the two events occurred *as well as* those in between].

In order to get "underneath" Peter's response to this event, we must first acquaint ourselves with a basic knowledge of the Jewish feasts—and in particular, their order. Each of the seven Jewish Feasts (or "appointed times" as God called them), inaugurated by God in the Old Testament, as well as having their own distinct purpose in the real-time lives of everyday Hebrews also possessed a prophetic dimension. Each festival fulfils a Messianic purpose in the future, ahead of the time they were first introduced. The first four have already been fulfilled and we await the fulfilment of the last three. Here they are, in order:

| Festival | Time of Year | Messianic Fulfillment |
|---|---|---|
| PESACH (Passover) | Spring | By Messiah's death. |
| HAG HAMATZOT (Unleavened Bread) | Spring | By the sinlessness of His blood offering. |
| HAG HABIKKURIM (Firstfruits) | Spring | By His resurrection. |
| SHAVOUT (Feast of weeks) | Sivan (7 weeks after Passover) | By the pouring out of the Spirit on believers. |
| ROSH HASHANA (Feast of Trumpets) | Autumn | By the rapture of the church. |
| YOM KIPPUR (The Day of Atonement) | Autumn | By The Day of Redemption (Second coming of Christ) |
| SUCCOTH (Tabernacles) | Autumn | By the dwelling of God with man—the 1000 year, "Millennial" Kingdom. |

Putting ourselves in Peter's shoes, we can deduce that his offer to make three shelters shows that he was clearly thinking of the Feast of Tabernacles where the Israelites were commanded to live in temporary "booths" or "tabernacles" for seven days for the purpose, as outlined in Leviticus...

> *...so that your descendants will know that I had the Israelites live in temporary shelters when I brought them out of Egypt. I am the L*ORD *YOUR* G*OD.* ~ Leviticus 23:43

But what triggered the thought of this feast in Peter's mind or did he truly simply not know what he was saying? To answer this, let us consider the *What? Where?* and *When?* surrounding this scenario.

First, *what* happened? We know that Moses and Elijah appeared with Yeshua. As leader of the Exodus from Egypt, Moses would have been an obvious link with the Feast of Tabernacles. Although it is impossible to know the precise extent of Peter's understanding of prophetic Scripture, it is clear from his question to Yeshua concerning Elijah immediately following this incident that he also connected Elijah to Tabernacles. *"Why then do the teachers of the law say that Elijah must come first?"* enquired Peter. Jesus replied, *"To be sure, Elijah comes and will restore all things"* (Matt. 17:10-11). From a Messianic Jew's perspective, the enigmatic phrase "restore all things" was a reference to the Millennial Kingdom where Elijah would "return" in the role of turning the children's hearts back to their fathers, in other words, reuniting the family around Messiah.

Regarding belief in Messiah, we know that Yeshua warned that His coming would split families right down

41

the middle in this age, and even leaving Messianic belief aside, Arnold Fruchtenbaum points out that the family has always been central to Jewish life but has suffered a decline in recent years. Elijah's ministry would specifically act to reverse this and his coming can be tied down to sometime before the Tribulation since Micah 4:5-6 tells us that God, *"...will send Elijah the prophet **before** the great and terrible day of the Lord."* From this we can deduce that Elijah will be resurrected sometime prior to the Tribulation to reunite Jewish families.

The sight of Elijah speaking with Yeshua must have resonated with Peter's end-times awareness even if the timing was wrong since Elijah was to come *prior* to the Tribulation which itself must *precede* the Kingdom, so Elijah and the Kingdom could not arrive simultaneously.

So it appears that Peter was aware of Elijah's future role in inaugurating the Millennial Kingdom. Interestingly, he would surely also have been aware of Zechariah 14 which tells us that the Feast of Tabernacles will still be celebrated in the Millennial Kingdom, enforced by divine prerogative.

Secondly, *where* did it happen? Tradition places the scene of the Transfiguration on Mount Tabor. However, the summit of Tabor was at that time occupied by a fortress, and the text gives no actual support to that tradition. The actual location is often considered to be one of the spurs of the snow-capped Hermon. Cæsarea Philippi, the last locality named prior to the transfiguration, lies under Hermon, and its glittering cone of snow may have prompted the expression, *"...exceeding white as snow,"* found in Mark 9:3 (from the KJV). In their attempt to describe the radiance of His clothes, different Bible translations and the other parallel accounts employ various alternative metaphors such as, *"white as lightning"*...and...*"whiter than anyone in the world could bleach them"*...almost as if there was no phrase truly strong enough to express the full potency of its brilliance.

The "high mountain" location of the transfiguration would have had additional links to Moses for Peter as it was on Mt. Sinai where the Law was received and where iconic elements of God's presence were encountered similar to those Peter had just witnessed, that is, clouds and voices emanating from God himself.

Peter may well have been aware that in the Millennial Kingdom, there will be a mountain—the biggest in the world upon which will sit the Millennial Temple and Millennial Jerusalem (not the New Jerusalem which is introduced at the end of the Millennial as part of what is sometimes called the *eternal order*). This mountain is referred to as *Jehoveh's House* (Isaiah 2:2) and will become the centre of Jewish worship according to Ezekiel 20:40-41.

Micah, a contemporary of Isaiah, states that Gentiles will also seek this mountain. According to Isaiah 4:5-6, the Shekhinah glory will completely cover the new Mount Zion in the form of a "cloud by day" just as it did Mount Sinai and the temporary Tabernacle in the wilderness wanderings with the obvious connections to Moses.

From Ezekiel, Peter may also have known that during the Millennial Kingdom, the world will be full of lush greenery and vegetation. If indeed he was cogniscient of this description, a sudden return to the familiar dust and stony landscape following the transfiguration must have been quite a let down and a sign that he had gotten ahead of himself!

Thirdly, *when* did it happen? Most commentators agree that these events can be reasonably placed approximately 6 months prior to the crucifixion, that is, the previous summer or autumn. Since the Feast took place in the autumn, Peter would have therefore felt the timing to be propitious for what he believed to be the ultimate fulfilment of Tabernacles. Today in Israel, on the last great day of the festival, the people dance with great joy while embracing the Torah Scrolls. *Zeman Simhatenu* is the rabbinic name for Succoth (Tabernacles) and means *"The Season of our Joy."*

All these icons—Moses, Elijah, Messiah, a mountain, a cloud, the Shekhinah glory, God's voice, the time of year, all conspired to lead Peter to an understandable but false conclusion about the ultimate fulfilment of the Feast of Tabernacles.

To be fair, Peter had just been told by Yeshua that *some who are standing here will not taste death before they see the Son of Man coming **in his kingdom*** (Matt. 16:28), and here he was seeing the Messiah in all His glory, a glory normally veiled in His humanity while on Earth. However, the real point is that from the table of Jewish Feasts, it is clear that Tabernacles comes *after* Passover and since the idea of the **suffering** servant was not at all well developed or accepted by the rabbis, then neither was Passover regarded as a Feast awaiting its ultimate fulfilment by Messiah's death, which is why Yeshua had to keep "pushing" this point home in an attempt to prepare His disciples for something that they would not have been expecting.

Although Peter's expectation was misguided in its timing, the text may in fact be hinting at a link between the transfiguration and the Messianic age even from the very first opening adverbial phrase, *"After six days..."* Psalm 90 states that, *"A thousand years in your sight are like a day..."* and from this, the Jewish sages derived the notion of a "divine day" of 1000 years duration. We also find an echo of this in Peter's words in 2 Peter, *"With the Lord **a day** is like a **thousand years**, and a **thousand years** are like a **day**."* A passage in the *Babylonian Talmud (Sanhedrin 97a, Rosh Hashana 31a)* demonstrates that some sages held to an argument which viewed the original creation week as a prophetic template for God's predetermined organization of time, spanning from when Adam received his soul to the end of Messiah's reign on Earth.

The argument goes that since man was made in the image of God and the Torah (in Genesis) describes six days of creation, followed by a day of divine rest (the Sabbath), then likewise, mankind has also been allotted six lots of 1000 years of "works" to do in the world followed by a 1000 year (Millennial) Shabbat (Sabbath). If this theory was in circulation at the time of the transfiguration, then this could well explain why the Gospel writers felt the need to record that telling phrase, *"After six days..."* (that is, on the *seventh day*). The reader is being primed, encouraged and "sign-posted" to see the One who was transfigured as He who would usher in this 1000 year Sabbath. And so once again, Yeshua's divine origins are brought into sharp relief.

45

*Then Peter came to Him and said,*

*"Lord, how often shall my brother*

*sin against me, and I forgive him?*

*Up to seven times?"*

*Jesus said to him, "I do not say to*

*you, up to seven times, but up to*

*seventy times seven.*

(Matthew 18:21)

# 70 X 7—JUST A BIG NUMBER?

> **Quick Summary!** Numbers in the Bible
> often mean something. In this passage, many
> have interpreted Yeshua to mean that our for-
> giveness of others should be unlimited. While
> this is undoubtedly true (because it is supported
> elsewhere), we notice that He could have
> chosen *any* large number to make this point—
> but didn't. Could there be a literal significance
> in the number 70 x7? Is there a "God pattern/
> principle" at work, which far from being a brand
> new teaching, is actually already embedded in
> the Hebrew Scriptures? There is even the hint of
> a future significance.

## And now in more detail...

How easy it is to read these verses and miss their deeper significance simply because of our disconnect with the Old Testament "God patterns" which Jews of that time would have spotted instantly! Peter, impulsive and short tempered by nature, asks Yeshua how many times he should forgive his brother. Before allowing Him to reply, Peter then suggests a reasonable quota, made all the more credible, he thinks, by his choice of seven which is, of course, God's chief "signature" number throughout Scripture. Yeshua, however, applies a factor of seventy to it resulting in a whopping 490 times! Without the advantage of an in-depth Old Testament knowledge, we all inevitably take this to mean that we must forgive very many, or even an unlimited number of times. However, the number "490" is not a randomly selected "big number" and possesses a much more fascinating pedigree.

For the Jew, every 7th day was a day of **Sabbath rest** (Exodus 20:10). Further to this, every 7th year was a known as a **Sabbath year**—an even greater rest. Moreover, 7 cycles of these 7th year Sabbaths was declared to be a **Jubilee Year**—7 x 7 years plus the following year (Leviticus 25:10-15). Leviticus tells us that this was to be a time when property would be returned to its original owner, slaves and prisoners freed, and debts cancelled. Already, we can start to see a link between Yeshua's **"70 x 7"** and the principle of **Jubilee** since 490 years is also 7 x 7 (that is, the Jubilee year) x10. So, to clarify, we have...

- The **Sabbath day** of rest (Every 7th day)
- The **Sabbath Year** (Every 7th Year)
- The **Jubilee year** (Once every 49/50 years, coming after 7 lots of the above)
- A "**Super Jubilee**"? (Lasting 490 years?)

The Sabbath Year, also known as the *Shemitah*, may have an application which, in recent times, has become widely discussed and popularized in books such as those written by Rabbi Jonathan Cahn and are useful for further study and investigation.

Peter would have immediately realized that Yeshua was saying in effect that the *Jubilee principle* of set times of unmerited grace and restoration to the undeserving was also to be the guiding principle in daily matters of fraternal forgiveness. The Jubilee connection would also have sharpened the rest of Yeshua's parable in Matthew 8 which focuses on, note, *the cancellation of debts*—a key Jubilee theme. But there is more...

If Yeshua was strongly alluding to the Jubilee cycle of grace, mercy, and debt cancellation, then might there be significance in the actual, literal number He cited which was 70 x 7... 490 years? Since the Hebrew Scriptures are based on *"God patterns"* (so well emphasized by Tom Bradford's *Torahclass.com*), might 490 years represent some kind of *"Super Jubilee Cycle"* of 49 x10 years? ...an extended period of time when Israel lived under God's general favour and acceptance? Answer—very possibly!...if we can find evidence in Scripture—and we can.

Returning to the central idea of a *Forgiveness Cycle*, the table on the next page illustrates that in fact, there are not just one, but four possible cycle candidates.

| Event markers | Duration | Adjustment | Total years |
|---|---|---|---|
| From the birth of Abram to the Exodus | 505 years | 15 years—the time from Ishmael's conception (Abram's "unauthorised" deviation from God's plan) to Isaac's birth—must be subtracted | 505 – 15 = 490 years |
| From the Exodus to the dedication of Solomon's Temple | 621 years | 131 years must be deducted to allow for the time Israel was in servitude to other nations under God's discipline as a result of their sin. | 621—131 = 490 years |
| From the dedication of Solomon's Temple to the Decree to Restore Jerusalem | 560 years | 70 years must be subtracted to allow for the time Israel (that is Judah) spent in captivity (judgment) in Babylon. | 560—70 = 490 years |
| From the Decree to Restore Jerusalem to the Death and Resurrection of Yeshua | 458 / 7 + 32 years | | 490 years |

[Note: If you investigate the above timings and dates, you may not reach the dates and durations which result in the 490 years "signature." This is because various corrective adjustments need to be made; for a fuller explanation of the times and dates used in the above table, I recommend the afore mentioned book, *Number in Scripture,* by E.W.Bullinger.]

On occasions, at the end of the 490 years of special grace and forgiveness, God did require payment for sins committed. This can be seen in the example (given in the table above), where God sent Judah (the southern kingdom of Israel) into captivity to Babylon for 70 years. The reason for this is simple: He had already said in the Torah that this would happen to them, and He intended to keep His Word. 2 Chronicles tells us that Judah had failed to observe the 7th Year Sabbaths by not "resting" the land as commanded by God for a full 490 years! Dividing 490 by 7 (because the Sabbath Year occurred in 7 year cycles) gives us 70 actual Sabbath years which had been missed and were thus "owed" to God and His land. Therefore, God decreed that 70 years was to be the appropriate punishment for the crime and while the land was vacated, it could finally, as 2 Chronicles 36:21 says ...*enjoy its sabbath rests.*

Curiously, these cycles may not even end here since, if there is any validity to the idea of forgiveness cycles, then we might expect them to continue on and re-emerge in the future at some point. Indeed, for those who hold to a literal 1000 year reign of Messiah on Earth immediately following the end of the tribulation (which many believe *is* Daniel's seventieth week), then this 1000 year period may also contain intriguing possibilities. We might be tempted to notice that 490 years fits into 1000 twice over but with a surplus 20 year discrepancy (1000 years—(490 x2) = 20 years).

At first sight, this discrepancy seems to render the math unpromising, but anyone who has researched the Jubilee Cycle will know that a degree of controversy surrounds the question as to whether or not it is a strictly 49 year cycle with the *49ᵗʰ year* being the year of Jubilee or a 49 year period with the *following 50ᵗʰ* year being the Year of Jubilee, representing a 50 year cycle but still based on a basic 49 year unit. This is known as *intercalation* (where an extra year is inserted). Basically, three possibilities exist: The Jubilee Year is either the 49ᵗʰ year, the 50ᵗʰ year, or the 50ᵗʰ year but with the 50ᵗʰ year acting as the first year of the next cycle. So, looking again at our elemental 490 year unit, this is 10 cycles of 49 years, 10 Biblical Jubilee Cycles.

So, we have 49 x10 = 490 years

Add 10 extra years (because there are ten 50ᵗʰ years) = 500

Double it for two cycles = 1000 years—the duration of The Millennial Reign of Messiah

Certainly there was a valid reason for the cessation of the previous 490 year cycle—Israel's rejection of Yeshua's atoning sacrifice and conversely, Isaiah 53, Zechariah 12, and others indicate that the trigger for the next "Forgiveness Cycle" will be Israel's national repentance, regeneration, and pleading for the Messiah's deliverance which will indeed trigger His immediate return followed by His 1000 year reign.

It must be remembered that these so-called "Great Forgiveness Cycles" are not referred to explicitly in Scripture, but they may be "observed" by those who, having grasped the *God patterns,* are then equipped to spot them when they appear in their various forms. Having said that these 490 year forgiveness cycles are not explicitly referred to in Scripture, it was, after all, Yeshua Himself who referred to forgiving seventy times seven—let he who has ears to hear...!

In conclusion, we can say that Yeshua's 70 x 7 demonstrates that He cited a Torah principle to underpin even personal forgiveness as shown by its connection with the Jubilee Forgiveness cycles. Curiously, the number *"490"* is never actually used in the Bible, it is always *seventy times seven* or *seventy sevens*. We are used to references being made to the root of a Hebrew *word*. Here, it seems that the number "7" is a root *number* which God likes to keep distinct. Further, we notice that another Torah tenet, the "ordinary" 7th day Sabbath was actually at the root of the whole structure of debt cancellation and forgiveness, reinforcing the huge importance which God gave to that day.

Jesus entered Jericho and was passing through. A man was there by the name of Zacchaeus; he was a chief tax collector and was wealthy. He wanted to see who Jesus was, but because he was short he could not see over the crowd. So he ran ahead and climbed a sycamore-fig tree to see him, since Jesus was coming that way.

When Jesus reached the spot, he looked up and said to him, "Zacchaeus, come down immediately. I must stay at your house today." So he came down at once and welcomed him gladly.

All the people saw this and began to mutter, "He has gone to be the guest of a sinner."

But Zacchaeus stood up and said to the Lord, "Look, Lord! Here and now I give half of my possessions to the poor, and if I have cheated anybody out of anything, I will pay back four times the amount.

Jesus said to him, "Today salvation has come to this house, because this man, too, is a son of Abraham. For the Son of Man came to seek and to save the lost."

(Luke 19:1-10)

# RIGHT NAME—WRONG NATURE!

> **Quick Summary!** Like most Hebrew names, Zacchaeus meant something. But more fascinating than that, is how he might have acquired his particular name; and there are other clues in the text which help bring him to life.

## And now in more detail...

Zacchaeus, the tree climbing short guy! Rabbi Daniel Thomson has discovered some fascinating connections to the cultural background of the time and it begins with a Jew called Hillel. It is generally believed that Hillel lived from around 110BCE to 10CE. He was one of the most important figures in Jewish history and founded the School of Hillel where the Jewish law would be studied. He was instrumental in developing the construction and organization of the texts of the Mishnah, which is the compilation of the commentaries of many Jewish sages on the laws of the Torah. This task was continued and added to after Hillel's death, including adding commentaries of later sages. The completion took another 200 years after Hillel's death. [The (Jerusalem)

Talmud contains the Mishnah and the Gemara, which is commentary on the *Mishnah* of many more Jewish sages over the next 200 years (300 for the Babylonian Talmud). (For more about Jewish sources, see the chapter "A Word about Jewish Sources.")]

Hillel had a young disciple called *Yohanan ben Zakkai* (which transliterates as *John son of Zakkai*). Yohanan was one of Hillel's most distinguished Rabbinic students, declaring him to be, "…the father of wisdom" and "of coming generations" Interestingly, *Yohanan* was known as the "*small* disciple", possibly from a diplomatic reference in the Babylonian Talmud (Sukkah 28b) calling him the "*lowest one*"[8]

When Hillel was lying on his death bed, his disciples came to visit him but Yohanan stayed outside by the door, whereupon Hillel called out "Where is the small Yohanan ben Zakkai?" As his most highly valued disciple, Hillel naturally wanted to see him before he died. Since *Yohanan* seemed to stay at the door initially, could it be that the others, being taller had surrounded Hillel's bed and *Yohanan ben Zakkai* stayed back knowing that he wouldn't get to see Hillel? This was probably a situation he had grown accustomed to. So we have a curious déjà vu here in that, just like the *Zacchaeus* of Luke's story, *Yohanan ben Zakkai* also had trouble seeing his great man! The precise source of this tradition referring to Yohanan ben Zakkai's height is elusive at this point but the staff at JewishEyes.org are well aware of the custom.

---

8 "Johanan was the least among Hillel's many pupils, 80 according to some traditions, 160 according to others. Nevertheless, Hillel (according to TJ and ARN2) singled Johanan out on his deathbed, calling him 'father of wisdom and father of the generations,'" Sefaria.org, http://www.sefaria.org/The_Fathers_According_to_Rabbi_Nathan?lang=en

Now, we know that parents through the ages like to name their children after famous national characters and Zacchaeus' parents may have been no different. The Jew Hillel was only a generation behind Zacchaeus' parents so could it be that our Zacchaeus of the Gospels, so diminutive in stature, was named after the great sage and scholar *Yohanan ben Zakkias*? Was Zacchaeus particularly small at birth which prompted his parents to portentously connect his physical features with their greatly revered sage and spiritual paragon? Zacchaeus' parents obviously had Godly aspirations for their son since not only was he named after the *father of wisdom* as Hillel called *Yohanan ben Zakkai,* but Zacchaeus' name means "pure" and "innocent."

Moreover, JewishEyes suggest the possibility of an actual familial link between the Gospel's Zacchaeus and Hillel's *"small Yohanan ben Zakkai"* which they base on the idea that "... If the early years of one who bears the name resembles the early years of the other who bears the name, it may be more difficult to argue against a connection."[9]

The ancient Jewish reference they use is from Sifre Deuteronomy chapter 357 where an overview of four characters' lives is made with the intention of drawing parallels:

> "Moses was 120 years of age when he died" (Dt.34:7). He is one of four who died at 120 years of age: And here they are: Moses, Hillel the Elder, Rabban Yohanan b. Zakkai, and R. Akiva.
>
> Moses lived in Egypt for forty years,and in Midian for forty years,and saw to Israel's needs for forty years.

9 Rabbi Daniel Thomson, from a video which is now lost to this author's memory.

Hillel the Elder ascended from Babylonia at the age of forty years, and attended sages [in discipleship] for forty years, and saw to Israel's needs for forty years.

Rabban Yohanan b. Zakkai was in business for forty years, and attended sages for forty years, and saw to Israel's needs for forty years.

R. Akiva began Torah-study at forty years, and attended sages for forty years,and saw to Israel's needs for forty years.[10]

To clarify, each sentence from their reference is best observed in the following manner:

| Character | First 40 Years | Second 40 Years | Third 40 Years |
|---|---|---|---|
| Moses | Spent forty years in Egypt. | Forty years in Midian. | Served Israel forty years. |
| Hillel the Elder | Came up from Babylon at the age of forty. | Attended (studied under) the Sages forty years. | Served Israel forty years. |
| R.Yohanan ben Zakkai | Engaged in business forty years. | Attended sages forty years. | Served Israel forty years. |
| Rabbi Akiba | Began Torah study at forty years. | Attended sages forty years. | Served Israel forty years. |

From this table, we can see the clear parallels between these men: secularism followed by preparation followed by service (to many of us, this sounds kind of familiar doesn't it?). JewishEyes suggest the delightful idea that there is some justification in considering our Gospel's Zacchaeus

---

10 *Sifre Deuteronomy,* pisqa'ot (chapter) 357:4, Fourth century AD, English translation by Professor Marty Jaffee 2016, Stroum Center for Jewish Studies, University of Washington, JewishStudies.washington. edu, http://jewishstudies.washington.edu/book/sifre-devarim/chapter/pisqa-357/

as following the same pattern since he too was engaged in commerce (tax collecting) similar to his name's sake:

| Character | First 40 Years | Second 40 Years | Third 40 Years |
|---|---|---|---|
| Zacchaeus of Luke's Gospel | ...engaged in commerce (tax collecting)... | ...repented... (and became Torah observant...?) | ...and served Israel? |

And so we do have parallels between both their names *and* their lives which, to JewishEyes, suggests the possibility that Luke's Zacchaeus could have been a son or grandson of Yohanan ben Zakkai.

We can imagine the heartache of Zacchaeus' parents as they longed for their son to live up to the name with which they had, in prophetic hope, endowed him—and when Yeshua found him, he had a long way to go! *JewishEncylcopedia. com* states that Yohanan ben Zakkai "was scrupulously ethical in all his dealings and behavior. He taught that the best character attribute a man could possess is a good heart, which he believed included all other virtues."[11]

In stark contrast, not only did Zacchaeus operate for the ruling Gentile occupiers as one of the hated traitor/tax-collectors, but from the text of Scripture, he also virtually confessed to extortion, rendering him doubly culpable and deserving of rejection from a Jewish perspective! Not only was Zacchaeus wealthy on the backs of the Jewish people, but Luke says he was a *chief* tax collector—*the only* man identified as such in the entire Bible. The disparity between his aspirational name and the reality of the corrupt betrayal

---

11 "JOHANAN B. ZAKKAI," JewishEncyclopedia.com, http://www. jewishencyclopedia.com/articles/8724-johanan-b-zakkai

59

of his own people could hardly have been greater. So all-in-all, there was plenty for his parents to lament!

Coincidentally, not only had *Zacchaeus* apparently not lived up to his (possible) name sake, *Yohanan ben Zakkai,* but he also seems to have missed the message of another *Yohanan ben Zakkai (John son of Zacharias),* more familiarly known to us as John the Baptist. Interestingly, the likely location of John's baptising activities in the Jordan is only around 9Km/5miles north of the Dead Sea. Coincidentally, Jericho, where Zacchaeus worked, is **in that same area** but slightly west of the Jordan so Zacchaeus surely **had every opportunity to take part in John's baptism had he so wished.**

This account in Luke makes it seem as though Yeshua entered Jericho **specifically to find Zacchaeus.** Notice that Luke says He entered but was apparently just ... *passing through.* There is a telling phrase, the truth of which will be appreciated by anyone who has ever worked under any sort of management, and it is this: management never **just** *passes through* ...Why? ...because they always have an agenda and Yeshua is no different in this respect. Notice also the **urgency** of Yeshua's words as He boldly invites Himself to Zacchaeus' house:

> *"Zacchaeus,* **come** *down* **immediately.** *I* **must** *stay at* **your** *house* **today.***" So he came down* **at once** *and welcomed him gladly.* (The Greek translated *must* is *dei* and means it is a real necessity).

These words sound very much like orders don't they? Did Zacchaeus have a military background of some kind, perhaps by defecting? At first sight, such a notion would seem unlikely to say the least. However, the Historian and scholar, Dr. Gerhard Falk, includes some fascinating comment on this subject in his online article, "It *Is* Jewish to Fight" thus:

> Before the rise of Christianity, **Jews were welcome soldiers and officers in the Roman armies** which had conquered the whole Mediterranean world. After the defeat of Israel by the Romans in the 70 C.E., the year of the destruction of Jerusalem, more Jews entered the Roman military service because Jewish fighting ability had been demonstrated by the tremendous courage of the defenders of Israel against the overwhelming Roman legions.[12]

And we know from Gospel references that the possibility of insurrection was taken very seriously by the Roman occupiers, which would support the view that they were regarded as extremely effective fighters. Although this is remarkable enough, Dr Falk goes on to link the end of this pragmatic relationship between the Jews and Romans with the beginning of anti-Semitism in Europe, thus:

> Then, when the emperor Constantine converted to Christianity and called the first ecumenical council in Nicea in 325 C.E., he decreed that Jews could no longer be employed as soldiers in the Roman armies because only Christians were welcome. Thus began that long history of anti-Jewish persecution in Europe together with the oft repeated adage that "it isn't Jewish to fight". The reason why this was

12 Dr. Gerhard Falk, "The Jewish Military Tradition: It *Is* Jewish to Fight!" Jewish Buffalo on the Web, jbuff.com, 3/22/01, http://jbuff.com/c032201.htm.

so commonly believed in both the Jewish and non-Jewish world was that Jews had no means of self – defence. Instead, Jews learned to survive for sixteen hundred years of persecution and brutality by using innumerable stratagems which were successful century in and century out in keeping the Jewish community alive.[13]

Having accepted the possibility of such Roman, militaristic pragmatism, then it becomes apparent that the peremptory manner in which Yeshua addressed Zacchaeus would have had echoes of a senior rank and therefore he might well have responded—and promptly! And might Zacchaeus have learned his extortion "trade" whilst serving in this military capacity; or, was it the other way round!?

It is interesting to note that even today, ex-police and service personnel are often favoured by town councils for positions such as town clerk; similarly, British private schools employ the same as their financial bursars—all positions connected to "holding the purse strings." If Zacchaeus had gained military experience as a defector, it may well be that the Roman occupiers favoured ex-military men as tax collectors as they would know how to successfully apply the necessary "unofficial pressure and persuasion" to reluctant tax debtors.

But the outcome of this story is often missed. Zacchaeus declared that *"...if I have cheated anybody out of anything, I will pay back four times the amount."* We tend to interpret this as being a meaningful gesture which demonstrates his repentance. This is of course true but why is it true? What if he had offered to pay back 2 times...or 3? Would that have

13 Ibid.

sufficed? On what basis did Yeshua commend Zacchaeus saying, *"Today salvation has come to this house, because this man, too, is a son of Abraham"*? Quite simply, the basis was Zacchaeus' return to *The Torah*—obedience to God's Law, the Law of Moses because Exodus 22:1 says that...

> *Whoever steals an ox or a sheep and slaughters it or sells it must pay back five head of cattle for the ox and **four** sheep for the sheep.*

We also see this principle applied in an incident in 2 Samuel 12:6 where we are told that...

> *...he must pay for that lamb **four times** over, because he did such a thing and had no pity.*

"Four" is significant in Bible numerology as it signifies *completeness*—but often a completeness which is specially related to the **earth**, for example, in Isaiah 11:12 and Genesis 13:14 which speak of the four directions, *"to the north, the south, the east and the west"* and *"the four quarters of the earth"* respectively. Indeed, the number four is used over 40 times in the book of Ezekiel, a book known for its (note) *material* descriptions of the future, millennial **Earth**. This connection with the earth is brought out in E.W.Bullinger's book, *Number in Scripture,* in which he points out that the 4th commandment is the first to mention the earth, while the 4th clause of the Lord's Prayer is also the first to mention the earth. In Genesis, the original material of creation was also completed on the 4th day, the 5th and 6th days being designated for the populating of the *materially complete* creation. [14]

---

14 Bullinger, pp. 84, 86.

However, another fascinating connection exists in the form of a comment made by Yohanan ben Zakkai himself. *Jewishvirtuallibrary.org* notes:

> Yohanan ben Zakkai's "method of minutely studying a biblical passage, inquiring into its motivation, and finding the grounds for some detail which he then converts into a universal idea transcending the specific context of the passage." [15]

They go on to say that, regarding Exodus 21:37:

> *"he shall pay five oxen for an ox, and **four sheep for a sheep**,"* Yohanan ben Zakkai said: "Come and see to what extent God shows consideration for the dignity of human beings. For an ox, which walks with its legs, the thief pays fivefold; for a sheep, since he carries it, he pays only fourfold" (Tosef., BK 7:10; Mekh., ed. Horowitz-Rabin, Nezikin, 12).[16]

This may be "a bit of a stretch" on his part since sheep also walk on legs but his ethical point is that a shepherd carries a sheep at times and so is one step down from an ox which never needs supporting but instead, is *self*-supporting as a beast of burden. The point is that if such sayings were known by the Gospel's Zacchaeus (possibly via his parents), then it may explain why his immediate pledge centred on a four-fold restitution since he had also thieved from the "sheep" of Israel.

It would be fascinating to know exactly what Zacchaeus understood about the significance of the number "4" but we cannot deny that he obviously believed that his application of that digit to a financial package would represent

15 "JOHANAN B. ZAKKAI."
16 Ibid.

material completeness as far as material compensation was concerned—and Yeshua certainly seemed to agree!

There is no mention of Zacchaeus coming to a realisation that Yeshua was the Messiah and so clearly, that issue is not intended as the focus here; rather, the trigger was Zacchaeus' repentance and that meant a return to Torah living.

This is slightly uncomfortable for many evangelicals as it seems to be linking salvation with works but that is really not the case. Like everyone, Zacchaeus was justified by faith, or rather, repentance and faith. In Matthew 3:8, John the Baptist said, *"Produce fruit in keeping with repentance. And do not begin to say to yourselves, "We have Abraham as our father...."* So Zacchaeus' spiritual status was restored as a true *son of Abraham* because his repentance was demonstrated by a return to the Torah. But faith is linked with repentance because Zacchaeus now had faith that following God's Torah—God's Law—was pleasing to God. Now Zacchaeus wanted to please God more than himself—which was the life he had been living up to that point.

In this respect, we notice that in inviting himself to the home of Zacchaeus, the crowd muttered that Yeshua was going to the house of a "sinner." This word is in some ways misleading as it is a Jewish idiom which means not necessarily a dreadful person in God's sight but simply someone who is not Torah observant, that is, does not follow the Law of Moses, or as we would say today, it really refers to *a secular Jew.* This reinforces the notion that Zacchaeus was not following God's Law in any meaningful way.

There is a very Jewish teaching "tool" being employed by Yeshua, one which, so-to-speak, is "invisible" to the naked eye and the modern word for this is *"remez,"* meaning to *hint* at something else beyond the face value and limits of what has been explicitly stated. In other words, it is what has not been said that becomes the focus as much as the actual words spoken. In the Zacchaeus narrative, Yeshua concludes with His mission statement, *"...for the son of man came to **seek** and to **save** the **lost**."* It seems highly likely that Yeshua had in mind Ezekiel 34. Notice verse 16, *"I will **search** for the **lost** and bring back the strays,"* and verse 22, *"I will **save** my flock."* Yeshua's words seem to be a composite of both verses, evidenced by the inclusion of the key words: **seek/search, lost,** and **save.**

Since Scripture was commonly known by heart, those present at the Zacchaeus incident would have immediately recognised that the **context** of His Ezekiel reference was God's continued love and concern for the lost "sheep" of Israel who had been failed by their leaders. So, from one concise phrase, Yeshua's audience was able to work out for themselves His hidden message(s) and application: that He Himself was the Shepherd who would search for and save His sheep (Ezekiel 34:11); to the leaders present, that they had failed in their task; and to Zacchaeus, one *of* the sheep, that God still loved and remembered him.

This use of "remez" is not well understood by modern believers since, although we can recognise when Yeshua is referring to the Old Testament, we have not been taught to appreciate the huge importance of other Scriptures, which **surround** these references in their original context. Like the proverbial iceberg, we must learn to peer beneath the surface features in order to come to a full appreciation of the whole.

Finally, the text tells us in Luke 19:11 that *While they were listening to this,* Yeshua further exploited the Zacchaeus encounter by using the money theme to go straight into the telling of *"The Parable of the 10 Minas."* In fact, we can only admire Yeshua's masterful handling of these "chance" encounters as he teaches not just on the theme of money, but very specifically, the theme of *"interest."* Using the techniques of *contrast* and telling parables to sustain the audience's attention, He compares the **negative financial interest** gained by dishonest means (the Zacchaeus story) to the **positive spiritual interest** which service to God's Messiah can "earn" (or perhaps a better word – "harvest").

NOTE: Readers may be interested to know that the Dr. Falk referred to in this chapter is the author of a book called, *The Jew in Christian Theology* (McFarland & Company, Inc., 1992), which traces the origins and history of Christian teachings about Jews. It includes the only English translation of Martin Luther's violently anti-Semitic booklet, *Vom Schem Hamphoras (Of the Hidden Name).*

*As he went along, he saw a man blind from birth. His disciples asked him, "Rabbi, who sinned, this man or his parents, that he was born blind?"*

*"Neither this man nor his parents sinned," said Jesus, "but this happened so that the works of God might be displayed in him. As long as it is day, we must do the works of him who sent me. Night is coming, when no one can work. While I am in the world, I am the light of the world."*

*After saying this, he spat on the ground, made some mud with the saliva, and put it on the man's eyes. "Go," he told him, "wash in the Pool of Siloam" (this word means "Sent"). So the man went and washed, and came home seeing.*

(John 9:1-7 KJV)

# SPIT: SPIRITUAL DNA?

Quick Summary! Yeshua often used strange methods to heal people—fingers were put in ears and spit rubbed on eyes. Many of us shrug our shoulders and put this down to God's ineffability and sovereign choice—He can heal any way He likes, we often conclude. But might this simply be our "best shot" resulting from a lack of cultural context. Is our default position "we **can't** know" actually a case of "we **don't** know"? Like everything Yeshua did, it had design, purpose, and message!

## And now in more detail...

Most of us have no problem with Yeshua laying hands on people to heal them, but the Gospel of John records that while in Jerusalem, Yeshua used spit to make mud which He then applied to a blind man's eyes. In Mark, He spat (directly) on another blind man's eyes to heal him. Elsewhere in Mark, we read that Yeshua inserted His spit-moistened fingers into a deaf man's ears while also touching his tongue with His saliva. So what is it with spit? Couldn't Yeshua simply have spoken the word or laid hands on these people in His more orthodox yet reliably successful manner?

The typical Gentile answer is that Yeshua, in His sovereignty as God incarnate, can choose what external means He wishes to heal and we must accept His will even though it may leave us baffled. However, a knowledge of the historical Jewish context provides us with a much more satisfying and "rational" explanation which, while diminishing the mystery element of Yeshua's actions, will actually enhance the cogency of His message and continuing theme of His mission which was, after all to present Himself to Israel as their appointed Messiah.

To understand Yeshua's actions, we first need to be aware of two traditions, which had become established by Yeshua's time. First, Arnold Fruchtenbaum (of *Ariel Ministries*) points out that Israel's leaders believed that when Messiah came, He would be capable of performing three specific miracles or signs which would serve to authenticate His Messiahship. These were: Healing a Jewish leper; healing a deaf and dumb demonised man; and **healing a man who had been blind from birth**. (In the healing we are discussing here, the man bears this out when he says, *"Nobody has ever heard of opening the eyes of a man born blind."*) These Messianic "signs" were not randomly selected but had a Judeo-Scriptural basis.

Firstly, why a *Jewish* leper? Because nowhere in Scripture has any Jew been healed of leprosy—Gentiles have, for example, Naaman the Syrian but no Israelites. (True it is that Moses' sister, Miriam became leprous but since this was a punishment, God's answer was not an

70

instant healing but rather, the command to follow the same cleansing procedure that was required as if her face had been spat on!)

Secondly, why a *demonised* deaf and dumb man? The standard Jewish procedure of driving out demons was to first establish verbal communication with the unclean spirit. (Notice Yeshua used the same approach.) In the case of a *deaf and dumb* person, this was obviously impossible which thus rendered the orthodox process impotent.

For the third sign, the man born blind carried with it the caveat—*from birth*—so as to remove any doubt as to whether his condition had simply been temporary and thus the healing natural, rather than supernatural and therefore divine. So this was the tick list the Jews expected Messiah to deliver in authentication of His messianic claims.

Moreover, in one of their newsletters, *Jewisheyes* describe a second tradition they believe to have been prevalent by the time of the second temple and Yeshua, reproduced here:

> It was conceivable in biblical times for a man to have several sons by different wives. Abraham sent away his wives and sons from Isaac so that there would be a clear demonstration of who was his heir. Occasionally one son would contest the claims of another as to who was the genuine heir. One reason for disputing the claim would be illegitimacy (whether the son was conceived within wedlock or not). The writer of Hebrews speaks of how we know that we are truly a child of G-d because we are disciplined by Him. An illegitimate son is not corrected in this way. Jewish tradition, taught that in matters of dispute with regard to inheritance,

G-d had a test which would supernaturally reveal who the legitimate son was; heir to the leadership birthright and family property inheritance. The people of the second Temple period were well aware of a tradition of the sages [Jewish scholars and teachers] which proclaimed that the saliva of a **legitimate, first born heir would have healing properties** against injury or disease. Once the disputed son's saliva anointed the affected member, healing was expected to miraculously take place if he was legitimate. [17]

Jewisheyes's commentary is likely to have been derived from the ancient Jewish source known as the Babylonian Talmud (Bava Batra 126b). One English translation of the passage sets it out as a kind of mini-play like this:

**Reuven:** I am sure that this man (Shichchas) is a firstborn.

**Rabbi Chanima:** How do you know?

**Reuven:** When people with eye-aches would come to his father, the father would tell them, *"Go to my son Shichchas. He is a firstborn, so his spit will heal you."*

**Question:** Perhaps he is a firstborn to his mother (but not to his father)!

**Answer:** If so, his spit would not heal."[9] [18]

So, things are beginning to hang together a little more now as clearly, in the minds of the Jews, there was a potent link between the power of a man's saliva and his origins or parentage. Of course, the question of Yeshua's parentage

---

17  Rabbi Daniel Thomson, *"Why Did Yeshua Use Spit to Heal?."* Newsletter, Vol. XII-Issue XVII, Apr. 22-28, 2007, Jewisheyes.org
18  Rabbi Arych Lebowitz, *"On the Daf: Bava Batra 126b,"* YUTorah, http://www.yutorah.org/daf.cfm/6025/bava%20batra/126/b/

and origins is probably the single most important issue which, understandably, preoccupied the Jews of the time as it was central to His Messianic claims. It was also central to Yeshua's teachings. In fact, it was Yeshua who raised the issue of His origins in this episode with the phrase, *"we must do the works of **Him who sent me**"*.

The *Jewisheyes* article continues...

Foremost among their concerns were questions about His parentage. After all, Yosef (Jospeh), Miriam (Mary) and Y'shua (Jesus) had freely acknowledged that Yosef was not Y'shua's father... and also that Miriam had never been married before she married Yosef. Yet, Y'shua clearly had been conceived and born... and someone had to be the father, but who?

Sadly, in today's society these facts would hardly raise an eyebrow. However, in that day it had all the makings of a horrible scandal with real lifelong ramifications. However, Y'shua also claimed that He had no earthly father... none whatsoever. He claimed to have come from the Heavenly Father, G-d. If He had been a sinner or the product of sin, **He could hardly be expected to be able to heal anyone, as G-d was the Source of all healing.** This is the context of John 8 and 9.[19]

Quite rightly, the article stresses that the "spitting issue," far from being a trivial and quirky curiosity is in fact very much in context with the previous chapter of John 8:

**A much larger lesson is at work here than simply a series of disjointed teachings and healings.** [19]

---

19 Rabbi Thomson.

And we find this in the Gospels; material is placed *where it is* for a reason—often to reinforce and integrate a deeper message...

> In chapter 8, Y'shua had spoken extensively about His origins, and when He spoke of His Father, the answer from his audience was, *"Who is **your** father?"* **It was no accident** that just after this exchange, in the same hour, He was asked the question, *"Who sinned—this man or **his parents** [*to bring about his blindness]?"* [20]

(We can see the trap the audience is setting itself—the corollary of their linking of sickness with illegitimacy should be that healing by (Yeshua) implies legitimacy!) The article continues...

> It was also believed by some that an **illegitimate** child would be chronically ill or have birth defects. He verbally answered the question of the origin of the blindness, but then demonstrated something which spoke convincingly about His own origins, His legitimacy and His right of inheritance. Y'shua chose to demonstrate that His saliva contained healing properties, presenting a "catch-22" to those who were His critics.
>
> According to the Sages, anyone whose saliva could heal in this way demonstrated by a supernatural revelation of G-d that He was the legitimate first born heir of His Father. How could His **earthly lack of a father,** yet the clear demonstration of **legitimate inheritance from Above** be reconciled? They could only be reconciled if His statements about His origins were true. The only true Heir of the Father,

---

20 Ibid.

legitimate and unsullied, the Source of healing and restoration.[21]

Notice also, that, subsequent to His use of spit, Yeshua sent the man to wash in the pool of Siloam, which John points out means "sent." So again, Yeshua is underscoring the theme of His origins in that He was *sent* by the Father. In actual fact, the link between the Hebrew term and the verb "sent" is dubious but that is not the point; Yeshua knew that that is what was commonly believed and so ***He exploited the custom in support of His Messianic claims.***
The article finishes by saying that...

...the conclusion of the story is both happy and sad. As with much of mankind, few choose to believe; most will not. The blind man believed, but the doubt expressed by others says they could not reconcile the conflict. *"We know that God spake unto Moses: as for this fellow, we know not **from whence he is.**"* His origins were still unresolved in their minds. His claim of legitimate inheritance, validated supernaturally by the Father, could not be reconciled with other things their ears had heard and their eyes had seen.
Proclaiming their ability to see clearly, they remained blinded to His person, His nature and His purpose.[22]

This excellent article and exposition points out that Yeshua's choice of spit as a healing medium was neither arbitrary nor baffling. He was doing what He often did— in His patience and mercy, He was prepared to use the

21 Ibid.
22 Ibid.

75

traditions and beliefs of His culture and time (whether actually true or not) to enable those present to come to the right conclusion regarding His divine parentage and position as sole legitimate heir to His Father's inheritance. This fits perfectly with John's overall purpose, which was to promote Yeshua's divinity. [Note also that he uses the word parent(s) six times in the passage.] Moreover, Yeshua performed two out of three special Messianic miracles (mentioned earlier) with the use of spit, thereby meeting the criteria the Jews *had themselves stipulated* as requisite for anyone claiming the Messiahship.

Since Yeshua did indeed fulfill their own criteria, they were, sadly, left without excuse and so in verse 41 He concludes with the inevitable judgment on the Pharisees, using a double meaning word play just to rub salt (or spit!) into their wounds:

> *"If you were blind, you would not be guilty of sin; but now that you claim you can see, your guilt remains."*

This chapter began with Yeshua's spit and ended with His *divinity*. However, for the sake of completeness, this would be an appropriate juncture from which to resolve the other component of Yeshua's identity, namely, His *humanity*. The dilemma is plain enough: The annunciation stories found in Matthew and Luke claim that Yeshua was conceived without a human father but later in the Gospel of Luke, Joseph is listed as Jesus' parent and father (Luke 2:27, 33, 48; 4:22). Indeed, through Joseph's lineage, Jesus is shown to have descended from King David (Luke 3:23–38). Do these accounts contradict the annunciation stories?

Our modern understanding of conception would state that for Yeshua to be fully human, He would have needed complete DNA. While Miriam (Mary) would have provided the X chromosome, who would have supplied the Y chromosome? Clearly, there are only two possibilities: God, or Yoseph (Joseph). But, since we know that it could not have come from Yoseph, then, our "X/Y" chromosome model might lead us to view a man with only one of these as necessarily only half male! Moreover—and to add insult to injury—the traditional way to explain Yoseph's passive role in all of this is to diminish his status to that of Yeshua's "adoptive" father.

To resolve these difficulties, an article by Andrew Lincoln—*How Babies Were made In Jesus Time* cited by the Biblical Archaeology Society (BAS)[10] —provides us with an important insight into the ancient Jewish mindset concerning conception, specifically, the differing contributions made by both sexes, concluding that the "one-parent-only issue" would not have been so troubling to the Gospel stories' ancient audiences. He writes:

> Their understanding of conception, shaped by a patriarchal culture, would have been some variation of the dominant Aristotelian theory. On this view, the male semen provides the formative principle for life. The female menstrual blood supplies the matter for the fetus, and the womb the medium for the semen's nurture. The man's seed transmits his logos (rational cause) and pneuma (vital heat/animating spirit), for which the woman's body is the receptacle. In this way the male functions as the active, efficient cause of reproduction, and the female functions as

the provider of the matter to which the male seed gives definition.[23]

Crucially, He concludes that...

In short, the **bodily substance** necessary for a human fetus comes from the mother, while the life force originates with the father.[24]

So the *material "stuff"* needed to build a body is provided by the mother, whilst the *"essence"* or *"spirit"* comes from the father. And therefore, The *BAS* note that...

Those who heard the nativity stories in Matthew and Luke would have considered Jesus to be fully human since **his mother supplied all of his bodily substance.** Lincoln clarifies: "In terms of ancient biology, **even without a human father,** Jesus would have been seen as **fully human.** His mother, Mary, provided his human substance, and in this case God, through the agency of the divine Spirit, supplied the animating principle instead of a human father." [25]

Lincoln points out that well known Greco-Roman biographies such as *Theseus, Romulus,* and *Alexander The Great* are all examples of stories where *the central character is given two conception stories, one natural and the other supernatural*, and that...

Dual conception stories for the same figure was not uncommon in Greco-Roman biographies, and Lincoln suggests that this was a way of **assigning**

---

23  Andrew Lincoln: "How Babies Were Made in Jesus' Time." *Biblical Archaeology Society*; Nov/Dec 2014.
24  Ibid.
25  Ibid.

**significance and worth to** those "who were perceived to have **achieved greatness in their later lives.**" In this genre, those who accomplished great things in their adult lives deserved an equally great—even supernatural—conception story.[26]

Of course, this is not to suggest that the Gospel writers simply crafted made-up stories of dual natural/supernatural conception to exploit their audiences familiarity with that genre; rather, it demonstrates, once again, the genius of God who was able to weave His plans into the prevailing culture of the day, which "just happened" to already be receptive— primed and ready—to accept an account of the God-man concept so central to the identity and origins of Messiah Yeshua—Jesus the Christ.

26 Ibid.

*Now when Jesus saw the multitudes about Him, He gave a command to depart to the other side [of the lake]. Then a certain scribe came and said to him, "Teacher, I will follow You wherever You go." And Jesus said to him, "Foxes have holes and birds of the air have nests, but the Son of Man has nowhere to lay His head." Then another of His disciples said to Him,* "Lord, **let me first go and bury my father**.*" But Jesus said to him, "Fol-low Me and **let the dead bury their own dead**.*"*

(Matthew 8:18-22, NKJV)

# A HARSH SAYING?

Quick Summary! When read without any background knowledge of past Jewish burial customs, most of us have inwardly squirmed with embarrassment at Yeshua's apparently harsh response to a sensitive situation. However, following some "digging" (dreadful pun!) into these, as well as the corrupt practices prevalent at the time, we realise that, most likely, the "boot is actually on the other foot" as the disciple in question may have been involved in a dangerous and prohibited business known as *"secondary burial."*

## And now in more detail...

This is a classic example of one of Yeshua's "harsh sayings" which seems to lack basic compassion in denying a man the opportunity to fulfil the fifth commandment by giving his father a proper burial. After all, even Elijah, often regarded as the austere counterpoint to his gentler acolyte Elisha, allowed him (Elisha) a brief return to his family following his initial calling by Elijah:

*...So he (Elijah) departed from there, and found Elisha the son of Shaphat, who was ploughing with twelve yoke of oxen before him, and he was with the twelfth. Then Elijah passed by him and threw his mantle on him. And he (Elisha) left the oxen and ran after Elijah, and said, "**Please let me kiss my father and my mother, and then I will follow you.**" And he (Elijah) said to him, "Go back again for what have I done to you?" So Elisha turned back from him, and took a yoke of oxen and slaughtered them and boiled their flesh, using the oxen's equipment, and gave it to the people, and they ate. Then he arose and followed Elijah and served him.* ~1 Kings 19:19-21 (NKJV)

So what on earth was Yeshua doing in our parallel story found in the Greek Scriptures? Of course, the majority interpretation is that Yeshua meant something akin to...

*"Let the spiritually dead bury the (already) dead—you should follow me and work to save those while they still can be saved."*

It seems that Yeshua is suffering from a bout of religious mania and is dumping love in preference for evangelical zeal. However, this typical habit by some Gentile commentators of attempting to "spiritualise" difficult texts often leads to inconsistencies, as indeed it does here. Byron McCane of Duke University, in his article entitled ***Let the Dead Bury Their Own Dead***, points to the oft neglected word "...*their OWN dead.*" It is clear that as far as Yeshua is concerned, *both* are *physically* dead![27]

---

27  Byron R. McCane, "Let the Dead Bury Their Own Dead: Secondary Burial and Matt 8:21–22," *Harvard Theological Review,* Volume 83, Issue 1, January 1990.

An examination of Jewish burial traditions however will enable us to make proper sense of what Yeshua was getting at. In first-century Judaism, a person who had just died was taken out and buried IMMEDIATELY in the family burial cave, which was normally hewn out of bedrock. We find this in the story of Ananias and Sapphira (Acts 5) where, "...*the young men arose and wrapped him* (Ananias) *up, carried him out* (immediately), *and buried him.*" Only a few hours later, Sapphira, having been similarly struck down was carried out by the young men who, "...*buried* (laid) *her **by*** (next to) *her husband* (in the cave)."

According to Jewish custom, immediately after a burial, the family would separate itself from the community and mourn for seven days. This mourning period was known as "sitting *shiv'ah*." Therefore, if this would-be disciple's father had just died, then how was it that he was in Yeshua's company at all since he should have been at home in mourning? We obviously have a paradox. Did Messiah harshly rebuke this disciple for merely wishing to follow the traditional burial custom, which would have delayed him only briefly?

## The Secondary Burial

To find a logical explanation which can resolve this paradox, we must examine further the Jewish burial practices at the time of Messiah.

In the online magazine, *Archaeology and Biblical Research*, Gordon Franz, in his 2009 article of the same title as Byron McCane's in which he even quotes McCane, reveals that:

After a body was placed in a burial cave, it was left to decompose. The family MOURNED FOR SEVEN DAYS. This initial mourning period was followed by a less intense 30-day period of mourning, called "Shloshim." However, the entire mourning period was not fully over until the flesh of the deceased had decomposed, usually about A YEAR LATER.[28]

The next step in the burial practice is explained by *The Jerusalem Talmud*...

When the flesh had wasted away, the bones were collected and placed in chests [known as ossuaries]. On that day [the son] mourned, but the following day he was glad, because his forebears rested from judgment (Moed Qatan 1:5).[29]

Gordon Franz again:

This final act of mourning, in which the fleshless bones were gathered and placed into a bone box called an ossuary, was known as the "ossilegium" or "**SECOND BURIAL.**" It was this act which invoked Yeshua's response. Yeshua's response to the disciple's request makes perfect sense when we consider the Jewish custom of SECONDARY BURIAL. Their fathers had died, been placed in the family burial cave, and the sons had sat shiv'ah (the first period of mourning) and most likely also shloshim (the second period). They then requested anywhere from a few weeks to up to 11 months to

28  Gordon Franz, "Let The Dead Bury Their Own Dead," *Archaeology and Biblical Research*, 2009, http://www.biblearchaeology.org/post/2009/03/20/Let-the-Dead-Bury-Their-Own-Dead.aspx
29  *Jerusalem Talmud*, Moed Qatan 1:5, c. 400 AD..

finish the ritual of ossilegium before they returned to Jesus. [30]

Thus, it seems plausible that our would-be disciple had completed his *shiv'ah* as well as *shloshim*; he was now looking for further leave of absence for up to one year while he monitored the status of his father's bones in preparation for the "**second** burial."

Gordon Franz sums up by saying that…

> We can also see that Yeshua's SHARP ANSWER fits well with the secondary burial idea. The fathers had been buried in the family burial caves and their bodies were slowly decomposing. In the tombs or burial caves (along with the fathers) were OTHER family members who had died—some awaiting secondary burial and others already placed in ossuaries. When Jesus stated "Let the dead bury their own dead," He was referring to the **TWO DIFFERENT KINDS OF DEAD** in the tombs: the bones of the deceased which had already been neatly placed in the ossuaries and the fathers who had yet to be *reburied"* Clearly, the little phrase *"OWN DEAD"* indicates that the fathers were included among the dead![31]

The *Archaeology and Biblical Research* article provides further valuable insight into the alarmingly heretical meaning into which this corrupt practice had evolved (or rather, descended!):

> The concept of gathering the bones of one's ancestors is deeply embedded in the Hebrew Scriptures

---

30 Franz.
31 Ibid. (Emphasis added.)

and reflected in Iron Age burial practices (Gen. 49:29; Judges 2:10; 16:31; I Kings 11:21, 43, etc.). However, by New Testament times, the concept had taken on a NEW MEANING.[32]

This article also contains this controversial statement:

> According to Rabbinic sources, the decomposition of the flesh **atoned for the sins of the dead person (a kind of purgatory)** and the FINAL STAGE of this process was gathering the bones and placing them in an ossuary (Meyers 1971: 80-85). Jesus confronted this CONTRARY THEOLOGY. Only faith in Christ's redemptive work on the Cross can atone for sin, not rotting flesh...Jesus may have rebuked this disciple rather harshly because he was FOLLOWING THE CORRUPT JEWISH PRACTICE OF SECONDARY BURIAL.[33]

So what is the evidence for this assertion concerning ancient Jewish beliefs regarding the afterlife? Many of us are unaware of the Jewish beliefs that were prevalent at the time of Yeshua so this may be a timely opportunity for a brief synopsis on the subject.

The idea of an intermediate state of the soul, release from which may be facilitated by the interceding prayers of others, is found, not in Scripture, but in the *Testament of Abraham*, an ancient, apocryphal-type text based on the Old Testament, generally dated to the latter part of the first century A.D. In this text, the description is given of a soul which, because its good and evil deeds are equal, has to undergo the process of purification (so as to "nudge" it

---

32 Ibid. (Emphasis added.)
33 Ibid. (Emphasis added.)

in the right direction) while remaining in a "middle state," and on whose behalf Abraham intercedes. The angels also join Abraham in his prayer, whereupon the soul can then be admitted into paradise.[34]

Furthermore, at the time of Yeshua, there lived a prominent Jewish scholar called *Shammai*. Contrary to *"The House of Hillel,"* who took a more liberal view of Scripture, *"The House of Shammai,"* (Shammai and his followers) subscribed to an uncompromisingly rigorous interpretation of Scripture and from an internet search for the book, *The Book of Jewish Wisdom: The Talmud of the Well-Considered Life* edited by Neusner and Neusner in the chapter *"The Justice of God"* we find the following:

> The House of Shammai say: [There will be] *three groups on the Day of Judgement* [when the dead will rise]; *one comprised of the thoroughly righteous; one comprised of the thoroughly wicked; and one of the middling* [people].[35]

Regarding the Scriptural basis for the belief in a "middling" group, in the same place, we also read...

> And concerning this group [that is, the middling group] David said (Ps 116:1): *I love the Lord, because he heard my voice* [and my supplications][36]

...which seems to suggest that the Shammaites believed this referred to David's prayers for those deceased who

---

34 Testament of Abraham; Recension A, xiv; c. 50-100 AD, http://www.earlyjewishwritings.com/testabraham.html
35 Jacob Neusner and M.M. Neusner, editors, *The Book of Jewish Wisdom: The Talmud of the Well-Considered Life,* Global Publications, Binghamton University, Binghamton, NY, 2001, page 137.
36 Ibid.

found themselves in this "middling" group, while another reference, this time to 1 Samuel 2:6...

And concerning this group, Hannah said: *"The Lord kills and brings to life. He brings down to Sheol and raises up."*... [37]

...would seem to most of us to be a clear evidence, not of a "middling group," but of a resurrection of Old Testament saints!

To be fair, a degree of theology could possibly be seen in the idea of purification resulting from decomposing flesh since it is true that, as the apostle Paul said, sin acts through the weakness of the flesh so... no flesh—no sin. One of the key achievements of the Jewish roots movement has been to restore the crucial importance of the *Old* Testament. However, this is an instance where we can thank God for the *New* Testament which is clear from Yeshua's teaching that only two groups exist: the sheep and the goats, whilst all the instruction which came after His death points to atonement by Messiah Yeshua's blood only. So, no "middling" group and no purgatorial intercession.

We can see this fascination with ancestral bones in Jacob when, as he lay dying pleaded with his son Joseph to *"carry me out of Egypt and **bury me in the burial place with my ancestors**."* Joseph, a good and conscientious son, promised to do so (Genesis 47:30). This is in contradiction to the Law of Moses and Yeshua who never had a good word for "messing" with tombs or bones:

*'Woe to you, teachers of the law and Pharisees, you hypocrites! You are like whitewashed tombs,*

37 Ibid.

*which look beautiful on the outside but on the in-*
*side **are full of the bones of the dead and ev-***
***erything unclean.***"      ~ Matthew 23:27

...And in Mark 5 we see that when Yeshua got out of the boat, He was met by a demon-possessed man *who came out of the tombs.* In fact, the man lived there. It is usually believed that he ended up there as a result of his unmanageable behaviour which, of course, may well be true. Was he a Gentile? Or was he a Jew who had been taken by boat and exiled to this Gentile region as a suitably "unclean" location for the dumping of hopeless cases? Alternatively, had he been involved in some form of the corrupt practices which have been discussed here and had taken himself off to these tombs? One thing is for sure: if he was a Jew, this man was in an unclean (and therefore *unauthorised*) zone; and if he was a Gentile, this still did not render the tombs an advisable place to be.

Notice also the link between bones which are **unclean** and the fact that the text refers to an **unclean** spirit; as Judge Judy of US TV fame says, *If you roll around in dirt, you get dirty!* Further, it is worth learning from Canon Jim Glennon who led the healing ministry of St Andrew's Cathedral, Sydney, Australia for many years.[38] Though a cautious and conservative Anglican who certainly did not "see demons behind every tree," he did encounter those who had attempted contact with the dead and lived to regret it! (So "Goths," other death cults, and religions which esteem

38 Fr David Chislett SSC, "Canon Jim Glennon - Healing, the Kingdom of God, and Stress," *Streams of the River Making Glad the City of God Blog,* Feb. 8, 2014, http://www.fministry.com/2014/02/canon-jim-glennon-healing-kingdom-of.html

bones and relics - beware!) Some may argue that this may well be a huge stretch of the speculative imagination but it is surely certain that this kind of problem was not without cause and, providing we draw a line between speculation and fact, it is a valid exercise to ponder and hypothesise using the information available.

Regarding contemporary beliefs about the degree of uncleanness of body parts and its persistence over time, the conclusions some rabbis came to are striking. B. R. McCane's book, *Roll Back the Stone,* includes a fascinating section from the Jewish writings which illustrates what extreme lengths some rabbinic thinking had gone to in their interpretation of Numbers 19:11, *"Whoever touches a human corpse will be unclean for seven days."* The passage in McCane's book comments on an ancient Jewish source pointing out that...

> An entire tractate (*m.'Ohal*) is devoted to the question of how far corpse impurity can travel and by what means. The rabbis concluded that it can travel almost indefinitely especially if nothing gets in the way. Direct physical contact is not necessary: corpse impurity can radiate outwards across shadows and through tiny openings. If, for example, someone walks so near a grave that his or her shadow falls upon it, corpse impurity instantly courses from the ground through the shadow and onto that person. As *m.'Ohal., 2:4* [39] puts it: *"The stone that seals a grave and its buttressing stone convey uncleanness by contact and by **overshadowing**."* [40]

---

39 Meaning: *Babylonian Mishnah* (m): Order: Toharot, tractate Ohalot 2:4.
40 Byron R. McCane, *Roll Back The Stone: Death and Burial in the World of Jesus,* Trinity Press International, Harrisburg, Pennsylvania, 2003, p. 71.

That being the case, the oft posed question about Yeshua's resurrection, *"Who moved the stone?" would* make more sense as *"Who would dare to even get within 100 yards of the thing*?!" This also explains why it was argued that tombs and graves should be located well outside towns and cities and, to guard against accidental defilement, annually marked with whitewash, which, we have now learned, may have also acted as an early warning system to allow the passer-by time to even assess the position of their shifting shadow relative to the grave!

In fact, McCane's description of impurity *radiating outwards* cannot help but prompt the modern reader to draw parallels between this ritual contagion and the contemporary hazard presented by (of all things) radioactive waste—a waste so toxic that it can pass through walls, spread contagiously to any number of people and contaminate the environment almost indefinitely. Both the ancient rabbi and the nuclear scientist would concur that the only viable disposal solution is to bury such toxicity under ground, label it with a visible warning...and keep well away! (In a sense, the potency of "dead men's bones" actually trumps that of nuclear waste since the latter *does* eventually decay whereas the former remains unclean indefinitely!) Interestingly, in 17 AD, one of Yeshua's enemies, Herod, built an impressive new capital city named Tiberius, after the contemporary emperor, only to discover that it was built on top of an old Jewish cemetery. It was said that **no pious Jew ever entered it**, and it was inhabited almost exclusively by Greeks and Romans.

This all serves to sharpen our appreciation of just how severe Yeshua's condemnation of the Pharisees was when he accused them of being *"..like **whitewashed tombs,** which look beautiful on the outside but on the inside are **full of dead men's bones and everything unclean"** (Matthew 23:27). Not only was He traducing their *internal condition,* but He was also alluding to their toxic effect on others.

So, returning to the theme of secondary burial, having appraised the best available Biblical archaeology, we are now in a position to come to a satisfactory conclusion. To this end, Franz in his *Archaeology and Biblical Research* article provides a useful interpretative, amplified, and paraphrased rendition of what Messiah's response might have otherwise looked like, now that we are better informed about these things, thus:

> *Look, you have already honoured your father by giving him a proper and decent burial in the family sepulchre. Now, instead of waiting for the flesh to decompose, which can **NEVER** atone for sin, go and preach the Kingdom of God and tell of the only true means of atonement—faith in and obedience to Christ. Let the bones of your dead father's ancestors gather his bones and place them in an ossuary. As for you, you follow Me!*[41]

[Notice here, the typical Hebraic use of a *physical impossibility* (the dead ancestors burying other dead) to illustrate a *theological impossibility* (the dead atoning for the dead)].

The astute observer may notice that Matthew's account identifies this potential disciple as a "scribe." Scribes were the professional intellectuals of the day. They knew The Law of Moses inside and out. So, we may ask, surely

---

41 Franz, "Let The Dead Bury Their Own Dead."

they of all people would be aware of these huge doctrinal errors! But, they were also so well educated that they began writing commentaries on the Law which took precedence over the Law itself. There were several thousand of these commentaries which provided rules for the Sabbath, tithing, and worship. By the time of Yeshua, the Scribes had strayed so far from the original Law with their personal interpretations, that what was taught was often nothing more than the traditions of men. This is one of the great pitfalls of intellectualism, or theological relativism—you can end up thinking you are smarter than God and begin "helping Him out" by grossly reinventing His Word to the point where it means something different or even opposite to that originally intended.

So, hopefully now, we have a more informed and sympathetic understanding of Yeshua's seemingly harsh response to that disciple. We can see that Yeshua was doing what He always did—upholding the Torah (the Law of Moses)—in this case, the command to honour your parents—while managing to differentiate between theologically corrupt practices (the second burial) and good Jewish custom (a traditionally prescribed period of mourning). This interpretation is therefore consistent theologically, Biblically, and historically.

*On the third day there was a wedding in Cana of Galilee, and the mother of Jesus was there. Now both Jesus and His disciples were invited to the wedding.*

(John 2:1-2)

# THE THIRD DAY—WHAT'S SPECIAL ABOUT IT?

Quick Summary! Sometimes the introduction leading into a story can contain details
that offer a door through which "hidden views"
may be glimpsed which will enrich our appreciation of the main narrative. The little phrase, "the
third day," though apparently a mere detail, can
be "unpacked" to such an extent that it may actually determine the theme of the entire story.

## And now in more detail...

Of course, the focus of this passage is usually Yeshua's
miracle of turning water into wine. But have you ever
noticed the very first phrase... *"On the third day"*? When
a seemingly superfluous detail is mentioned in the Bible, we
should always question whether it is indeed as insignificant
as it first appears. Again, a knowledge of Jewish customs
will enlighten us!

Surprisingly, we will find the origins of our answer in
the very first chapter of the first book in the Bible - Genesis,

where we find the creation narrative. If we were to present this in the form of a table, we notice something curious:

| The Day (as we call it) | The Day (as God called it) | God's comment on His work |
|---|---|---|
| Sunday | 1st day (Literally, Day 1) | …it was good. |
| Monday | 2nd day | |
| Tuesday | 3rd day | …it was good….*it was good.* |
| Wednesday | 4th day | …it was good. |
| Thursday | 5th day | …it was good. |
| Friday | 6th day | …it was good. |
| Saturday | 7th day | …it was very good. |

Whilst the 7th day understandably receives an intensified blessing, "…*it was very good*," as a summative overview of all God's works, Tuesday seems to have been randomly singled out for a favoured "double blessing." Moreover, this appears to have been at the expense of Monday which receives no approbation from the Maker at all! In attempting to solve this conundrum, the Jewish website, *Chabad.Org* offers the following comments from an ancient Jewish text called *Genesis Rabba* which is said to have been written in the third century AD[42]

> Why is '*that it was good*' not written in connections with the second day? … R. Samuel b. Nahman said: **Because the making of the waters was not finished [until the third day]**, whereas '*that it was good*' is applicable only to a completed

42 Assigned by tradition to the amora, Hoshaiah (Osha'yah), in Palestine. http://www.jewishencyclopedia.com/articles/3056-bereshit-rabbah

work: consequently *'for it was good'* is written twice
in connection with the third day, **once in respect
of the making of the waters and a second time
on account of the work done [completed] on
that [third] day.**[43]

[Another English translation (for which the source has
been lost) included these words: "an unfinished thing is not
in its fullness and its goodness."]

Whatever the correct explanation is, Jewish custom
does hold to certain months and days as being especially
auspicious for a wedding—Tuesday (the third day) is
certainly considered one of those highly favoured as a day
which carries with it a "double blessing." No wonder then,
that in his account of the wedding in Cana, John mentions
*"Yom Shloshi"* (the third day - Tuesday) since the happy
couple did indeed receive a "double blessing"—the wedding
itself and the attendance of Messiah along with his gift of at
least 120 gallons of the finest wine!

However, the third day "enigma" does not end there
as there is a further symbolic and numinous significance,
astutely observed and commented upon by Daniel Egan of
the *Bible Tidbits* website, in his January 29, 2009 post. The
insights on the next two pages are based partially on his
article.[44] He points out that John 1:1 (NIV) starts with...

*In the beginning was the Word and the Word was
with God and the Word was God. He was with*

43 Genesis Rabba Bereshith 4:6, page 31 in the online English translation
   at Archive.org/stream/RabbaGenesis: https://archive.org/stream/
   RabbaGenesis/midrashrabbahgen027557mbp#page/n77/mode/2up

44 Daniel Egan, "The Gospel of John and a New Creation," Bibletidbits.
   blogspot.com, 1-29-2017, http://bibletidbits.blogspot.com/2009/01/
   gospel-of-john-and-new-creation.html

*God in the beginning. Through him all things were made; without him nothing was made that has been made.*

Clearly, John is alluding to the beginning of the original creation week. Significantly, this motif continues throughout Chapter 1 with a quick check of the NIV Bible showing John beginning each new section with the words — *"The next day..."* It is almost as if John is constructing his own **parallel creation week**, not in the sense of creating a complimentary or supplementary account but rather to reinforce his message of (Messiah) Yeshua's divinity by implicating Him in God's original creation.

So by the end of the first 28 verses of John 1, we not only have a parallel with the original creation but John also creates His own *"Day 1"* (when light was created) by repeatedly using the word *"light"* (**7 times** note!). Then there follows **three** uses of the phrase *"The next day"* which brings us to *"Day 4."* John 2 then immediately begins with the phrase *"On the third day..."* If by now, our "whiskers are twitching" and we are on the lookout for confirmation of what John is up to, then we might well be tempted to combine *"Day 4"* with *"On the third day"* by taking this as the third day on from *"Day 4"* which makes *"Day 7,"* which neatly terminates his parallel *"creation week."* Therefore, the wedding takes place both on the **3rd day** (an actual *Tuesday*) and the **7**$^{th}$ **day** in John's parallel "week" system.

This may be highly significant as there is a belief in Judaism that God has correlated the **six days of creation plus one Sabbath day** with the total time allotted to mankind on earth as being **6000 years (of "works") + a**

***1000 year Millennial (Sabbath rest).*** (This is more fully discussed in the chapter "Right Festival—Wrong Order"). The salient point here is that by linking the wedding to John's parallel 7<sup>th</sup> day, John is pointing to Yeshua as being the bridegroom "to be" since, according to Arnold Fruchtenbaum, Messiah's Millennial reign actually begins with His ***wedding feast.*** In fact, it is notable that what we call "the wedding in Cana" in actual fact, centers on the wedding ***feast.*** Notice also that the theme of both the 3<sup>rd</sup> day of creation *and* the wedding in Cana is the ***gathering of water.***

Regarding the six jars, we notice that John identifies them as stone—not clay. These vessels were, as John states, *"the kind used by the Jews for ceremonial washing."* But why stone? Wouldn't clay be much easier from which to make a water container? Surely, it must be a whole lot easier than hacking away for hours with a bolster and lump hammer? But there is indeed a good reason for this which trumps the "effort" aspect. Due to clay's natural porosity, if a clay jar were to become ritually contaminated in some way (Lev. 15:12), it would need to be broken, as it was, so-to-speak, beyond redemption, unlike stone which did not "absorb" contamination; hence the use of stone.

Fascinatingly, there is confirmation of a link between John's parallel "days" and ritual contamination as cited in Numbers 19:11ff. For instance, in Numbers 19:11-13 which tells us that,

> *Whoever touches a human corpse will be unclean for seven days. They must purify themselves **with the water** on the **third day** and on the **seventh***

*day; then they will be clean. But if they do not purify themselves on the **third** and **seventh** days, they will not be clean. If they fail to purify themselves after touching a human corpse, they defile the LORD'S tabernacle. They must be cut off from Israel. Because the water of cleansing has not been sprinkled on them, they are unclean; their uncleanness remains on them.*

...And verse 17 says that...

*For the unclean person, put **some ashes** from the burned purification offering into a jar and pour fresh water over them.*

The ashes referred to above were the ashes of the red heifer sacrifice and would be mixed with water. Washing with this concoction made the unclean person clean again. It is well known from Jewish writings that samples of ash, as well as being stored in the Temple in Jerusalem, were kept at various locations in the wider community so that anyone coming into contact with a dead body could go through the purification procedure locally without necessitating an inconvenient return to Jerusalem. Also, if these jars were for red heifer ash purification then, once filled, if some of it was used, it was forbidden to refill the jar with new water—it all had to be used and then a fresh quantity made up—no cheeky diluting or other short cuts were permitted!

In other words, such was the seriousness and holiness of this purifying agent, that, in modern parlance, the message would have been—don't mess with this...at all! Therefore, in filling these jars with water and then "messing" with the jars' contents and purpose in a way which was clearly supernatural, Yeshua was proving Himself to have an authority beyond human, in other words—divine.

But there is yet more. Why is this extraordinary event not referred to as a *miracle* but rather, in John 2 as *"... the first of Yeshua's **signs**."* Enter Moses! We know from Deuteronomy that Moses said that God would send *"...a prophet like unto me"* and judging by the number of times that Yeshua's actions in some way paralleled those of Moses, we can tell just how esteemed Moses was in the eyes of the common Hebrew not to mention, in some sense at least, God Himself. Exodus 7 tells us that God performed *"signs"* through Moses for Pharaoh and the *first* sign (note the Cana link) was turning water into blood. Sounds familiar doesn't it? Moreover, the text says that this would appear, *"in vessels of wood and in **vessels of stone"** —just like the wedding in Cana! The sign then was, quite simply that the prophet who was to come—the "second Moses" —had!

And there is more still! In the ancient Jewish commentary known as the Gemara (which is part of the Mishnah), in Ketubot 111b, we find a delightful description of the unlimited abundance of wine in the Messianic Era. Based on the passage in Genesis 49:11 about the Messiah tying his donkey to the vine, (*"He will tether his donkey to a vine, his colt to the choicest branch"*), it was said that grapevines will be so fruitful that a city's supply of wine will come from a single vine, the stalk will be used as firewood, and that the fruit will be so large that a single massive grape could be stored in one's house and used as a wine-cask is used today. Wine enthusiasts will be further encouraged by the use of 'homer' – a measure of volume equivalent to 220 litres!

This is what the sages understood by Micah 4 which states that, *"Everyone will sit under their own vine and under their own fig tree, and no one will make them afraid."* This is taken as meaning that at that time, there will be no want, each individual (not just the rich) will not only have all the wine (vine) and food (fig-tree) that they could ever want, but that it will come easily and without toil (everyone will *sit*) and be enjoyed in peace, without fear of attack from enemies. The conversion of water into prodigious libations of top quality wine at Cana would have nicely balanced the **backward**-looking reference to Moses with the **forward**-looking allusion to the Messianic Kingdom which was, and of course remains, in the future.

In fact, in the previous chapter of John's Gospel—John 1, we see the calling of Nathaniel who seemed easily won over just by Yeshua's simple statement, *"I saw you while you were still under the fig tree."* It was customary to meditate on and learn Scripture while sitting under the dappled shade of a tree and Yeshua's reference to the fig tree certainly seems to have triggered an unusually spontaneously full-blooded response from Nathanael resulting in his "wow" declaration— *"Rabbi, you are the Son of God; you are the king of Israel."* And from a Jewish perspective, when Nathanael used the term "King of Israel," he certainly would have had this golden age in mind when foreign rulers would be expelled and Messiah would reign supreme.

Arnold Fruchtenbaum of Ariel ministries has a fascinating and very plausible "take" on Nathanael's declaration. He points out that when Yeshua sees Nathanael coming, He remarks, *"Here is a true Israelite in whom there is no deceit* (or *guile*, depending on your translation)." Following Nathanael's declaration, Yeshua told him that he would see *"heaven open and angels ascending and descending..."* Notice the three give-aways—Israelite, deceit, and angels ascending and descending. Who had their name changed to "Israel'? Who was known as a deceitful trickster? Who saw heaven open and angels ascending and descending? Clearly, it is the story of Jacob. Arnold Fruchtenbaum suggests that in all likelihood, Nathanael had been meditating on the story of Jacob under the fig tree, so when Yeshua said to Nathanael *"Here is an Israelite in whom there is no deceit,"* he was letting Nathanael know that He had basically read his mind——hence, his immediate "shock and awe" declaration of Yeshua's divine origins!

What do these ideas about the wedding at Cana teach us? When we approach a highly cultural Biblical event such as a wedding from a Jewish perspective, then rather than skimming the text, we are able to appreciate the full significance of what happened and why. It is the difference between examining a diamond ring from a "bird's eye" view and picking it up, rotating it back and forth to catch every facet and angle of its sparkling brilliance. Ultimately, our appreciation of the jeweller Himself will grow as we marvel at the One who has cut so many facets into this short story. Hopefully, we are now, so to speak, a few more facets the wiser.

*"Come to me, all you who are weary and burdened, and I will give you rest. Take my yoke upon you and learn from me, for I am gentle and humble in heart, and you will find rest for your souls. For **my yoke** is easy and my burden is light."*

(Matthew 11:30)

# THE YOKE OF HEAVEN

**Quick Summary!** The expression "my yoke" is derived from the Jewish phrase "the yoke of Heaven." This referred to the specific way that a particular Jewish teacher would interpret the Law of Moses so as to teach others the law's requirements. It may seem that Yeshua was implying that the Torah was too difficult to live by and so He was offering an easier alternative. However, He was actually *supporting* the Torah by offering the correct interpretation which linked the external with the internal "self"...and which was the "do-able" version which God Himself originally intentioned.

## And now in more detail...

This little phrase—my yoke—is an interesting one, worthy of closer attention as it has been the subject of much misunderstanding. Our common understanding of this "yoke" idea is that the Law of Moses was a burden, which no one could keep with the accompanying implication that the God of the Hebrew Scriptures was unfair and cruel, heaping endless commandments upon His people just to provide

Him with an excuse to condemn them for their inevitable failures. We then interpret Yeshua's words in the passage above as meaning that He, in contrast had come to do away with all that and replace it with a much easier and "softer" alternative. But is this really the case?

Was the Law of Moses impossible to keep? Was Yeshua really so different from the God of the Hebrew Scriptures? To answer this, let us look at what God Himself said about the Law He was giving when He gave it...

> *Now what I am commanding you today is **not too difficult for you** or beyond your reach. It is not up in heaven, so that you have to ask, "Who will ascend into heaven to get it and proclaim it to us so we may obey it?" Nor is it beyond the sea, so that you have to ask, "Who will cross the sea to get it and proclaim it to us so we may obey it?" No, the word is very near you; it is in your mouth and in your heart so you may obey it.*
> ~ Deuteronomy 30:11-14

So, clearly, from God's point of view anyway, He gave the Law so that it *would be* obeyed because it *could be* obeyed! And, not only was it possible to keep, it was not too difficult—perhaps even reasonably easy—not a burden requiring masses of wearisome effort.

Now compare these sentiments to Yeshua's words above (page 104); do they not begin to sound pretty close? ...quite similar?...that Yeshua and the God of the Hebrew Scriptures are in fact, singing from the same hymn sheet? But if this is the case, why did Yeshua feel the need to "promote" His burden as being light, and that His yoke was easy. It is as if

the version promulgated by the ruling classes of Scribes and
Pharisees was certainly not easy or light! To understand
this, we need to understand the concept of "the yoke."

The Jewish sages had an expression known as—
"accepting the yoke of Heaven."[45] To grasp this idea,
Rabbi Moshe ben Asher draws our attention to the first
commandment back in Exodus 20:2...

> "I am the Lord your God, who brought you out of
> Egypt, out of the land of slavery."

Now, you may be thinking, "hang on a minute, this is
only the opening pronouncement—the first commandment
is in the next verse, verse 2, *You shall have no other gods
before you.*" But that is exactly the point; since there are
two forms of the first word "I": one, "*ani,*" calls our attention
to the **speaker**, making it an announcement whereas the
other, "*anochi*" (used in this verse) conveys the idea of a
special, intimate relationship between the speaker and the
one being **spoken to**.[46] So, in our translations, the rather
blunt, dominant sounding phrase, "*I am the Lord you God*"—
an announcement—actually becomes, "*I am to be the Lord
your God*"—a commandment/invitation—not a relationship
that already is, but rather, a relationship which puts the
onus on the people asking the question, "***What must we do
for the Lord to be our God?***" Put another way, we could say
that...

45 "...Rabbi Akiva [b. 50 AD] teaches us the importance of accepting
   the yoke of Heaven...." *Mishna order: Zera'im (Seeds), tractate:
   Berakhot* 61b, https://www.sefaria.org/Berakhot.61b?lang=bi
46 Rabbi Moshe ben Asher, Ph.D. and Magidah Khulda bat Sarah,
   "The Yoke of the Kingdom of Heaven," *Khevra shel Kharakim*, 2007,
   gatherthepeople.org, http://www.gatherthepeople.org/Downloads/
   KINGDOMS_YOKE.pdf

*...the basis of our relationship with this God is not to be how we feel about God or what we want from God, but on what God wants from us.*

... and it is this idea that the sages called "accepting the yoke of Heaven."

So, the yoke which Yeshua was "advertising" as easy and light was quite simply, the Law of Moses—the Torah—*but, the correct interpretation* of the Law which would then result in the Law being an easy and light burden to keep. The problem was that like every law that has ever been written down, some interpretation is inevitably required to apply those laws into everyday situations. Since the Torah was given around 1400 years before Yeshua's birth, there had been an awful lot of interpretation! This often involved constructing what rabbis call "fences" around the Law.

"Fencing a commandment" works like this: Take the commandment from Exodus 23, *"Do not cook a young goat in its mother's milk."* Cooking a young goat in its mother's milk was a pagan, Canaanite practice so God obviously did not want the Israelites to copy this. However, somebody soon spots a problem: What if you are cooking a young goat in milk? There is a tiny chance that the milk you are using came from that young goat's mother. Answer? Erect a "fence" around the commandment by adjusting it so that it now reads, *"Do not cook a young goat in milk (of any sort)."* So now, the new commandment seems safer than the original.

But then someone else spots another problem: What if you are eating goat from a plate which just might have been in contact with milk from a mother goat which might, possibly have been the mother of the young goat on your plate? Answer? Erect another "fence" so-to-speak, "further out" from the previous one; this will make the original commandment safer still. In this case, have two entirely separate sets of plates—one for dairy and one for everything else.

Clearly, although the original intention of the fence was a genuine concern to protect the commandment by making it harder to break either deliberately or accidentally, there is always another fence that can be erected. In this case, what is next? To eat goat raw? Prohibit goat entirely? None of that was ever God's original intention.

So in our example here, the fences incrementally morphed the original commandment until they had ultimately nullified God's simple, original commandment. This is what is known as the "oral law," the extra "fences," twists, turns, adjustments to the original commandments, which had been passed on and added to throughout generations. This is what Yeshua meant when, in criticising some of the Pharisees in Mark 7:8, He said...

> *"Thus you **nullify** the word of God **by your tra-***
> ***dition that you have handed down.** And you*
> *do many things like that."*

Notice that Yeshua's contention was not that the Law had to be interpreted to make it applicable to real life situations since, as already stated, all laws need that. Rather, it was the elevation of those man-made interpretations above the Law itself which He called "nullifying" the Law. Interestingly, since the original intention of a "fence" was a good one, we also find that Yeshua erected His own fences. For instance, let us look at Matthew 5 where Yeshua says...

*"You have heard that it was said, 'You shall not commit adultery.' **But I tell you** that anyone who looks at a woman lustfully has already committed adultery with her in his heart."*

Many of us have interpreted this passage as another nail in the coffin of the Law of Moses as Yeshua seems to be adding to, or modifying the original commandment, *"You shall not commit adultery"* by use of the phrase, *"But I tell you."* However, He is really just erecting a "fence" to protect it, by implying that the actual deed begins with the thought. He is saying that the Pharisees' focus on external observance was flawed since adultery (the end result) is the effect of a cause—which is the unseen thought. Like an iceberg, nine tenths of breaking the commandment is what is going on in the heart. Yeshua was leading His audience to an *undivided* model of "self" where the outer is an honest representation of the inner.

Further, if you have read the section in this book called "Authority—Jewish Style!", you will know that the standard method of Jewish teaching was to quote a string of other rabbis in support of your opinion, a "Rabbi So-and-so says that Rabbi So-and-so said that..." type of approach. Notice though, that in the passage above, Yeshua breaks with this tradition by making it clear that He stood on His own authority—*"But I tell you."* This was radical and highly controversial since He was claiming to have personal authority to interpret the Law of Moses without recourse to the endorsement of others.

Returning to our original theme, this then was His "Yoke of Heaven"—His own particular interpretation of the

Law of Moses: not full of endless add-ons and burdensome man-made traditions but which sought simply to unite the external with the internal, in a way which perfectly expressed God's original purpose 1400 years earlier.

And, just as a kind of postscript on the theme of the "Yoke of Heaven," take a look at these three passages. First, God's words when giving the Law (as previously quoted)...

*Now what I am commanding you today is not too difficult for you or beyond your reach. It is not up in heaven, so that you have to ask, "Who will ascend into heaven to get it and proclaim it to us so we may obey it?" Nor is it beyond the sea, so that you have to ask, "Who will **cross the sea** to get it and proclaim it to us so we may obey it?" No, the word is very near you; it is in your mouth and in your heart so you may obey it.*

~ Deuteronomy 30:11-14

Secondly, Yeshua's words in Matthew 23:15...

*"Woe to you, teachers of the law and Pharisees, you hypocrites! You **travel over land and sea** to win a single convert, and when you have succeeded, you make them twice as much a child of hell as you are".*

And finally, a summary of what is known as *The Gilgamesh Epic*...

Gilgamesh is an epic about the adventures and character development of a young king endowed with superhuman powers. It is similar to later epics such as Homer's "Iliad" and "Odyssey" in several ways. For example, Gilgamesh and the Iliad each center on a hero with extraordinary physical prowess. (In

111

the Iliad, the superman is Achilles). Moreover, in Gilgamesh and the Odyssey, each main character fights monsters, crosses seas, and visits mysterious lands. In all three epics, mythological gods play a major role, but the settings are in real lands—Gilgamesh in Mesopotamia (in present-day Iraq), the Iliad in and just outside the walled city of Troy (in present-day Turkey), and the Odyssey in countries and islands in the Mediterranean region.[47]

This is a nice example of Yeshua using stories that were well known to His audience to help convey His message. The *Gilgamesh Epic* is an epic poem dating to about 2100 BC so it had clearly been known for hundreds of years before the Law was given and thousands of years prior to the time of Yeshua. Due to its fame, Yeshua vilifies the Pharisees' "Yoke of Heaven" (their interpretation of the Law) by comparing them to Gilgamesh who, according to the epic, makes a long and perilous journey *over land and sea* to find the secret of eternal life. The relevance of this epic to the Pharisees would have been striking: Yeshua is saying that the Pharisees have assumed the role of "Gilgameshes," believing themselves imbued with supernatural powers from on high for their heroic quest to, in their case, deliver the secret of eternal life to others.

The truth though, He says, is that instead of teaching the new disciple the correct "Yoke of *Heaven*," rather, they would make him twice as much a son of *Hell* as they were by inculcating them with doctrines based, not on God's statutes and mercy, but on legalism, hypocrisy, and self-

---

47 "The Gilgamesh Epic," *Cumming Study Guides*, cummingsstudyguides.net, https://www.cummingsstudyguides.net/Guides6/Gilgamesh.html

righteousness. Furthermore, the "secret of eternal life," was standing literally right in front of them in the form of the "Living Torah"—Yeshua. The Pharisees were in the privileged position to see a literal fulfilment of God's words (in the Deuteronomy 30 passage), where God says not to look *"...beyond the sea, so that you have to ask, 'Who will **cross the sea** to get it and proclaim it to us so we may obey it?' No, the word is very near you."* Indeed, the "Word"—Yeshua— was literally very near to them, though sadly they remained blind to that fact.

*Now early in the morning He came again into the temple, and all the people came to Him; and He sat down and taught them. Then the scribes and Pharisees brought to Him a woman caught in adultery. And when they had set her in the midst, they said to Him, "Teacher, this woman was caught in adultery, in the very act. Now Moses, in the law, commanded us that such should be stoned. But what do You say?" This they said, testing Him, that they might have something of which to accuse Him. But Jesus stooped down and wrote on the ground with His finger, as though He did not hear.*

*So when they continued asking Him, He raised Himself up and said to them, "He who is without sin among you, let him throw a stone at her first." And again He stooped down and wrote on the ground. Then those who heard it, being convicted by their conscience, went out one by one, beginning with the oldest even to the last. And Jesus was left alone, and the woman standing in the midst. When Jesus had raised Himself up and saw no one but the woman, He said to her, "Woman, where are those accusers of yours? Has no one condemned you?"*

*She said, "No one, Lord."*

*And Jesus said to her, "Neither do I condemn you; go and sin no more"*

(John 8:1-12)

# THE WOMAN CAUGHT IN ADULTERY—A LET OFF?

**Quick Summary!** Most Christians view this episode as Yeshua revealing the "nicer" side of God by letting off a sinful woman who, according to the Law of Moses should have been executed. The Law of Moses is seen as unreasonably harsh and as much the guilty party as the woman herself. However, a proper examination of the circumstances surrounding the event says otherwise. In truth, Yeshua manages to demonstrate God's mercy while upholding the righteous requirements of the Law.

## And now in more detail...

Being so familiar, we assume the intended meaning here to be obvious: do not judge. Yeshua had come to do away with the Mosaic Law's systemic harshness and replace it with grace. In this particular episode, the woman caught in adultery gets "let off" from the Mosaic penalty of execution by the grace of Yeshua.

However, this is based on a serious misunderstanding that the God of the Old Testament was intolerant, judgmental, and unforgiving, in contradiction to Yeshua who came to demonstrate God's hitherto concealed "nicer" side. This belief spawns two further and related misconceptions: Firstly, the Old Testament is semi (if not totally) redundant; and secondly, Yeshua is thus free to make up His own rules, resulting, in this particular case, in the guilty being "let off."

But how can this be? We know that Yeshua was not on a mission to expurgate the Law of Moses from Matthew 5:18 which states that, "*until heaven and earth disappear, not the smallest letter, not the least stroke of a pen, will by any means disappear from the Law until everything is accomplished.*" Notice also that the Scripture says they were, "*...testing him, that they might have something with which to accuse him.*" Of what were they trying to accuse Him? Answer: What they were always trying to accuse Him of—breaking the Mosaic Law, and as usual, He was not going to fall into the trap. With this in mind then, could it be that actually, the Law of Moses saved the woman?

The crucial point here around which all else revolves, is that regarding matters of the Mosaic Law, the entire 613 commandments were always known as **The Law**, not **The Laws** (plural). That is, where a number of laws pertained to any particular situation, that cluster of laws operated as a *whole*, in other words *due process* was crucial to satisfying God's justice system and failure to follow that process was also sinful as stated. That God sees the constituent components of the Mosaic Law as "***morally irreducible***" is also clearly demonstrated by James who says that, "*For whoever keeps the whole law and yet stumbles **at just one point** is guilty of breaking all of it* " (James 2:10). Since, according to 1 John 3:4, breaking God's Law is sin, then those attending the scene were also guilty of sin for the following reasons:

Firstly, Deut. 17:6-7 states that on:

> *...the testimony of two or three witnesses a person is to be put to death, but no one is to be put to death on the testimony of only one witness. The hands of the witnesses must be the first in putting that person to death, and then the hands of all the people.*

But there is no mention of any specific witnesses, just an allegation that the woman was caught in the act.

Secondly, Deut. 22:22 indicts the man as well as the woman (it takes two to tango!) by commanding that, *"If a man is found sleeping with another man's wife, **both the man who slept with her and the woman must die.** You must purge the evil from Israel."* Since the commandment is clear that both parties are equally culpable, where is the man? Since the accusers claim that they caught her in the act, then so must he have been, but again, there is no mention of him.

Thirdly, Deut. 19:16-20 states that...

> *If a malicious witness takes the stand to accuse someone of a crime, the two people involved in the dispute must stand in the presence of the Lord before the priests and the judges who are in office at the time. The judges must make a thorough investigation, and if the witness proves to be a liar, giving false testimony against a fellow Israelite, then do to the false witness as that witness intended to do to the other party. You must purge the evil from*

*among you. The rest of the people will hear of this and be afraid, and never again will such an evil thing be done among you.*

Since the male counterpart to the accusation was not also in custody and being similarly charged along with the woman then clearly a *"thorough investigation"* had not been conducted as commanded in Deuteronomy 19. We know from Proverbs 6:16-19 that the Lord *detests a lying tongue... hands that shed innocent blood* (e.g. unjust stoning)...*a false witness...*, and especially appropriate to this situation, *those who stir up conflict in the community!* Of course, the accusers seemed far more interested in trapping Yeshua than paying attention to the **due legal process**; not surprising since the law made it clear that a false accusation could result in the **accusers receiving the same penalty as the falsely accused**!

Though brutal, stoning by the two witnesses, followed by the remainder of the community when seen from a Jewish frame of reference, did at least provide a form of "witness protection" by spreading the responsibility across the entire community rather than focusing it on just a couple of witnesses; an important consideration in a tribal-clan system where vendettas and retaliation in the form of honour killings by the aggrieved family would have been likely were the execution carried out by a limited number of specific, identifiable individuals.

Yeshua's words *"Let he who is without sin cast the first stone"* is normally taken to mean that we are all sinners in a general sense and so are in no position to judge others. This is the crucial point across which the truth has been "bent" because from Yeshua's frame of reference (the Law of Moses), He is referring to the *specific* sin of adultery. He is not contradicting the Law of Moses on this matter which certainly does *permit a judgment* to be made *providing certain criteria have been met.* Rather, He is drawing out the witnesses' own internal condition, (their malicious motivations and hypocrisy rather than a love for justice and God's Law) as being highly relevant to administering the Law's penalty for adultery. The spiritual or moral aspect had already been enshrined in Jewish law for 1500 years. But where were the witnesses anyway? Only a mob was present with no witnesses identifying themselves. Noticeably, it was the older men who dropped their stones and departed first, they being more scripturally knowledgeable and thus, either quicker to realise the weakness of their position…or were they actually guilty of the same sin?

This is a further point, made by Arnold Fruchtenbaum of *Ariel Ministries* who says that the Pharisees had an interpretation of the point of law in Deuteronomy 19:18, which may have been highly pertinent to this situation. Dr Fruchtenbaum maintains that "false witness" included the concept that those actually *doing* the accusing *must not be guilty of the same sin as the accused.* This interpretation seems to arise from a broader or fuller understanding of what it means to be a "false witness" which includes not just fabricating evidence but also invalidating the accuser's moral imperative to pass judgment when they themselves are guilty of the very same sin. Dr Fruchtenbaum derives this idea from Talmudic sources, available in his latest volumes of *Yeshua, The Life of Messiah from a Messianic Perspective.* [48]

Although this is a pharisaic-Jewish and not scriptural interpretation of that law, it is not a bad one at all when cross-referenced with the consistent anti-hypocrisy thrust of Scripture, not to mention Yeshua's own words regarding the principle of removing the log from your own eye before taking the specks out of others'. The apostle Sha'ul (Paul) certainly believed this and was uncompromisingly specific on the matter as demonstrated in Romans 2:1:

*"You, therefore, have no excuse, you who pass judgment on someone else, for at whatever point you judge another, you are condemning yourself...,"*

Why?...

*"...because you who pass judgment **do the same things.**"*

And later in the same chapter:

*"You who say that people should not commit adultery, do you commit adultery?"*

Since everyone seemed keen to wander off immediately following Yeshua's permission to cast the first stone—***provided they were without sin***—what might this say regarding the crowd's own guilt of adultery?!

Yeshua's parting comment, *"Neither do I condemn you"* is also consistent with the Law of Moses, as there were no witnesses present anymore and not having witnessed the act Himself, Yeshua, in His humanity was also not in a

48 Arnold G. Fruchtenbaum, *Yeshua, The Life of Messiah from a Messianic Perspective.* Vol. 3, Ariel Ministries, 2017, p. 25.

position to condemn the woman, despite knowing her guilt, hence the admonition "...*go and **sin no more***." It was not so much a "let off" as "case dismissed." Furthermore, although the legal punishment for adultery seems brutal to us, by the very nature of this sin, the safeguards of two or more witnesses being required surely meant that the majority of cases must have either been dismissed or never even known about.

On the subject of what Yeshua wrote with His finger, much has been said, most of which must necessarily be pure speculation. The real point however is often missed; the emphasis is on *finger*, not on what He wrote. Only ten of the Law's 613 commands were written by the "finger" of God, commonly known as the Ten Commandments and one of them was *"You shall not commit adultery."* The rest were dictated indirectly through the mediator Moses. Yeshua may have been making the symbolic point that He, with God, was the Law's co-author and is thus fully qualified to interpret it correctly. In fact, in everything pertaining to the Law, Yeshua's mission was to demonstrate the Law's correct interpretation in practice, perfectly exemplified in this story where a sinful woman found grace and mercy in Yeshua and the Law of Moses.

So far, so good. But, Rabbi Daniel Thomson of *Jewisheyes. org* has a different, or at least, additional "take" on this story by examining the context in which it occurs, specifically, the timing. The story takes place on the day following the final 8th day of the autumn feast of Sukkot (or Tabernacles). It was on the last and greatest day of the festival that, "Jesus stood and said in a loud voice, *"Let anyone who is thirsty come to me and drink. Whoever believes in me, as Scripture has said, rivers of living water will flow from within them"* (John 7:37). Yeshua had timed this announcement—invitation—perfectly to coincide with the Jews' traditional water-pouring ceremony, one of the festival's high points. That water was fetched from the Pool of Shiloach (Siloam) which itself comes from the famous Gihon spring. One of the favourite Scriptures to be read at this time was from Jeremiah:

> *A glorious throne, exalted from the beginning, is the place of our sanctuary. L*ORD*, you are the hope of Israel; all who forsake you will be put to shame.* ***Those who turn away from you will be written in the dust*** *because they have forsaken the L*ORD*, the spring of living water.*
> ~ Jeremiah 17:12-13

The spring/ river of living water is of course Yeshua, as He had just announced (in John 7:37). Since the purpose of this whole incident was to trap and ultimately kill Yeshua, He is presenting the Jeremiah quote as a prophecy fulfilled since the context is one of condemnation.

Thus, the Rabbi proposes that with all this symbolism and Scripture uppermost in their mind from the recent festival, it seems more than a little plausible that Yeshua bent down and wrote ***the names of those present*** who a) had come to discredit Him, and  b) were violating the Law of Moses. Gathering around Him as He wrote, they may well have been disturbed to see their own names appear and with Jeremiah 17 still ringing in their ears from the recent festival, were beginning to feel on very shaky ground. [49]

Although the phrase "the finger *of God*" is not actually used in John's record, it is certainly implied, given John's overall theme of Yeshua's divinity. The 19th century teacher Rabbi Tzvi Hirsch Kalisher taught that the expression "finger of God" means something "...that is not doubted— that its *essence, quality, and intentions are clear*,"[22] meaning, it is clearly evident that God's hand is in it.[50] If this *was* the meaning behind this rarely used expression, then the salutary u-turn—condemners to the condemned— which Yeshua effected upon the participants must have come as quite a shock!

Rabbi Thomson also makes the point that the woman's guilt was by no means certain even though Yeshua told her to "*Go and sin no more*" since, although falling short of adultery *per se*, suspicious or inappropriate behaviour towards the opposite sex was seen as sinful in itself and it may well have been this that Yeshua was referring to when he dismissed her. [51]

The problem with the traditional interpretation of this story is that it tends to reinforce the false distinction between the God of the Old Testament (hard and unforgiving) with the Jesus of the new (loving and merciful). Closer ex-

49  Rabbi Daniel Thomson, Gospels and The Acts Through JewishEyes, JKB 1024; Vayikra, JKB Series, mp3 Download, 01hr:50mins, *Jewisheyes.org*
50  Rabbi Tzvi Hirsch Kalisher, "The Finger of God—Ki Tisa, Torah Portion," quoted from his *Sefer haBrit,* JewishJournal.com. Accessed Jan. 2017.
51  Rabbi Thomson, "Gospels and The Acts Through Jewish Eyes," JKB 1024; Vayikra, JKB Series, mp3 Download, 1hr:50mins, *Jewisheyes.org*

amination reveals that Jesus was in fact acting consistently with the Law of Moses, which, after all, should not surprise us *when viewed from a Jewish frame of reference.* Jesus did not invent a new soft and fuzzy way to contradict the Law of Moses so as to "let people off" but *was* able to demonstrate God's mercy while fully satisfying the righteous demands of the Law. (Does this remind you of another one of Yeshua's significant acts?)

The bad news is that this story is a classic example of our Gentile understanding superimposing itself over a Jewish context resulting in guesswork, supposition, and even error. The good news is that when seen from a Jewish perspective, apparent and uncomfortable discrepancies between the God of the Old Testament and the Jesus of the New, simply disappear.

NOTE: Rabbi Daniel Thomson describes a further Torah principle which is relevant to this incident (Video Lesson: "Shelach"; June 11-17, 2017 / 7-23 Sivan 5777). He states that he who should be first to cast the first stone is the injured party, that is, the woman's husband. At that point, he is acting as the "avenger of blood", or *Goel.* In Hebrew, *Goel* can be translated as either the "avenger of blood" or the "kinsman redeemer." There is a Messianic picture here as Yeshua came once as the kinsman redeemer but will come again to avenge Israel's blood by warring against the nations; in an otherwise downbeat narrative, this Messianic allusion is welcome. The rabbi further explains that the severity of the punishment for adultery stems from marriage being a depiction of the God (male) + Israel (female) covenant; as such, overlooking adultery would be to sanction Israel switching to false gods — the most egregious sin for a Jew.

*And so I tell you, every kind of sin*

*and slander can be forgiven,*

*but blasphemy against the Spirit*

*will not be forgiven.*

*Anyone who speaks a word against*

*the Son of Man will be forgiven,*

*but anyone who speaks against the*

*Holy Spirit will not be forgiven,*

*either in this age*

*or in the age to come.*

(Matthew 12:31-32)

# UNFORGIVABLY UNREPEATABLE!—WHY?

Quick Summary! Most Christians have, at some point, asked themselves the question, *"Have I committed the sin known as "blasphemy against the Holy Spirit"?"* Of course, to answer that convincingly, you have to know what it is! A wide variety of explanations have been put forward in an attempt to answer this particularly thorny issue. The definition proposed by the Jewish-American *"Ariel Ministries"* is different because it ties it down to a specific set of circumstances which are now impossible to reproduce.

## And now in more detail...

Such is the confusion and uncertainty concerning the identity of the sin referred to by Yeshua as *"the blasphemy of the Holy Spirit"* that guilt-anxiety over whether or not they could have committed it has almost become a rite of passage for all new believers! The vast majority of possibilities suggested as to the identity of this specific sin are Gentile, not Jewish interpretations. But should not our Jewish brothers and sisters in Yeshua be the ones to whom we might naturally turn when the going gets tough in the text? In particular, the Hebrew scholar and American Jew, Arnold Fruchtenbaum of Ariel Ministries, by using a mix of Jewish cultural background, Scriptural context, and "out-of-the-box" thinking has elegantly resolved this perplexing issue. Let us then, investigate this matter with reference to these three components.

Firstly then, the **Jewish cultural background**. The incident which led up to the "blasphemy" issue involved the healing of a demon-possessed man, blind and mute. Jewish tradition of the time held that when Messiah came, He would demonstrate His authenticity by performing three unique Messianic miracles. In his recent book, *Yeshua, The Life of Messiah from a Messianic Jewish Perspective,* Dr Arnold Fruchtenbaum writes:

> It should be stated that the general ability to perform signs and wonders is not unique to Yeshua. During the time of Moses and the days of Elijah and Elisha, God worked through miracles; people were healed and the dead were raised. So these were not miracles unique to Yeshua. Elijah and Elisha both worked such wonders (1 Kings 17; 2 Kings 4). However, the divine purpose of the signs and wonders Moses, Elijah and Elisha performed were different. They were to authenticate the prophetic calling of these men, but when these prophets performed them, no one asked, "Can this be the Messiah?" Just so, when Yeshua performed the same miracles, the people glorified God, saying **A great prophet** is arisen among us: and, God has visited his people (Luke 7). However, the Scriptures show that **He performed some miracles that**

128

**were uniquely different, and their purpose was to authenticate His Messiahship.**[52]

So Dr Fruchtenbaum is suggesting that there existed in the Jewish mind-set a special group of Messiah-authenticating miracles and that this can be deduced, not from ancient sources, but largely from the unique outcomes which resulted from these specific events. In the healing incident just preceding the whole "blasphemy" passage, we note that the man in question was the recipient of at least one and possibly two of these Messianic signs, namely, healing a man *born blind* and healing a man who was demon possessed *and mute*:

> *Then they brought him a demon-possessed man who was blind and mute, and Jesus healed him, so that he could both talk and see. All the people were astonished and said, "Could this be **the Son of David?**"* ~ Matthew 12:22

That it was the pharisaic leadership, and not ordinary people, who are in focus here is clear from the text immediately following:

> *But when **the Pharisees** heard this, they said, "It is only by Beelzebul (sic), the prince of demons, that this fellow drives out demons."* ~ Matthew 12:24

We can see that the people were still undecided about Yeshua and it was the Pharisees who were holding them back. But why was this particular healing the trigger for such a vehement response from Yeshua in Matthew 12?

---

52 Arnold G. Fruchtenbaum, *Yeshua, The Life of Messiah from a Messianic Perspective*, Vol. 1, p.143.

This can be answered by referring to this Jewish belief that when Messiah came he would perform three specific miracles. One of these was the casting out of a *dumb demon.* The Jewish procedure for casting out demons was to first make vocal contact with the demon. In the case of a dumb demon, this would be impossible and therefore, to the Jewish way of thinking, healing such a case would only ever be possible by Messiah Himself.

But we can also deduce the uniqueness of this miracle from the crowd's reaction. Notice Luke 4:36 tells us that the people were astonished, *"...for with power and authority he commands the unclean spirits, and they come out."* Now compare this response to that which followed the Matthew 12 dumb demon incident where we find, again, that the people were astonished but then added the question, *"Can this be **the Son of David?**"*—a Messianic title. Clearly, in the people's minds, *this* miracle had the effect of immediately "promoting" Yeshua into a different league, from prophet to a serious contender for Messiah.

The particular difficulty associated with dumb demons also explains the Mark 9:29 incident where a man brought his mute son to the disciples but who were then unable to heal him. Yeshua told the disciples that, *"...**this kind** come out only by prayer."* But to **what kind** was He referring? Simply, the specific kind that do not speak.

Another Messianic miracle was healing someone who had been blind *from birth*. Being *born* blind was important as the Jews would investigate any healing carefully to establish whether the man had been suffering from a blindness-causing condition which was only temporary. If this were so, then it was possible that the condition had simply healed naturally which would of course, invalidate any claim by the healer to possess Messianic powers. Although obviously not Scripture, the apocryphal book of Tobit does report alleged healings of the blind and so the common culture of the time did not regard this specific healing as special proof of Messiahship.

However, there is no record of anyone who was *born* blind being healed, as evidenced in John's Gospel, Chapter 9:32 where we find that, *"Since the world began, **it was never heard** that anyone opened the eyes of a man **born** blind."* And, from the disciples original question, *"Rabbi, who sinned, this man or his parents that he was born blind"*—we can see why; if a man's blindness was God's punishment for sin, then what chance was there of healing him? Moreover, should it even be attempted? Surely then, went the logic, only God Himself could overturn and reverse such divinely ordained judgments. Clearly, this view was also prevalent among the Pharisees whose acerbic retort—*"You were altogether born in sins"*—left the man in no doubt as to who *they* thought was to blame.

In his article, "The Three Messianic Miracles," Arnold Fructenbaum discusses this more fully. So to the third Messianic miracle: the healing of a Jewish leper. In brief, Dr Fruchtenbaum observes that in the Hebrew Bible, three Jews were afflicted with leprosy as a result of divine judgment: Miriam (Moses' sister); Gehazi (Elisha's servant); and Uriah or Azariah, King of Judah. Not surprisingly then, leprosy became associated with God's judgment and, indeed, since the Mosaic Law was completed in Deuteronomy 31, as far as is known, no Jew has ever been healed of leprosy.[53]

---

53 Arnold Fruchtenbaum, "The Three Messianic Miracles," *Messianic Bible Study #035*, Ariel Ministries, San Antonio, Texas, 1983, 2005, http://

In fact, Yeshua Himself confirmed that there were many lepers in the day of Elisha but only Naaman the Syrian (not Jewish) was healed.

In Mark 1:45, the people's reaction to the healing of a leper was that, "...*As a result, Jesus could no longer enter a town openly*" such was the excitement caused. Even more impressively, the narrative immediately following this incident finds Yeshua teaching and healing in Capernaum, about 3 days journey from Jerusalem. Luke 5:17 tells us that present were teachers and Pharisees who "...*had come from every village of Galilee and from Judea and Jerusalem.*" Dr Fruchtenbaum points out that these were no mere local teachers but rather the leading intelligentsia who had arrived from Jerusalem which, we notice, is where the man would have gone to fulfill the procedure required for cleansed lepers when seeking an official "clean bill of health." Clearly, this healing had had a uniquely invigorating effect on the people and their leaders. Dr Fruchtenbaum notes that when Yeshua instructed the man to do this, as per the Law of Moses, He added the additional phrase, "...*as a testimony to them* (the priests)." But a testimony to what... or whom? A testimony to His claims of Messiahship.[54]

So, the point here is that Yeshua had just demonstrated His Messianic authenticity by performing signs, which the Jews *themselves* considered **legitimate proof of Messiahship**—but instead of believing in Him, decided **to ascribe the healing to Satan!** This is why the Pharisees' response to this specific miracle so antagonised Yeshua.

www.messianicassociation.org/ezine48-af-three-messianic-miracles.htm
54 Ibid.

Having established the importance of these "stand-out" proofs of Messiahship, if we now apply the principle of *"context is king,"* then something obvious will leap out at us. Notice the recurrent use of one specific word found in the immediate context of the episode that provoked Yeshua's use of the blasphemy phrase. Here are the instances (all in Matthew):

> *"A wicked and adulterous **generation** asks for a sign"* (12:39).

> *"The men of Nineveh will stand up at the judgment with **this generation** and condemn it"* (12:41).

> *"The Queen of the South will rise at the judgment with **this generation** and condemn it"* (12:42).

> *"That is how it will be with this wicked **generation**"* (12:45).

> *"A wicked and adulterous **generation** looks for a sign"* (16:4).

> *"You unbelieving and perverse **generation**."* (17:17).

Although there are four instances where the word generation is used in connection with the blasphemy issue, if we extrapolate the passage to take in those usages which continue the theme of a wicked and adulterous generation, it is significant that there are *six* such instances. Six is the number of Godless man, corrupted motives and of falling short. Yeshua may well have been linking the Pharisees with the lineage of murderous Cain, whose recorded *generations* (that word again) abruptly stop after only *six generations*. Similarly, Yeshua was accused by His accusers *six* times of having a demon.

133

This continued emphasis is clearly significant. Although Yeshua does say that "*anyone* (that is, any individual) *who speaks against the Holy Spirit will not be forgiven,*" His condemnation which follows in the "Sign of Jonah" passage rubs in the fact that it is *this generation* which is guilty of it and will thus suffer for it. Notice also, that Yeshua provides examples from history of people—Gentile peoples at that—who were notoriously guilty of great sin yet did not commit blasphemy of the Holy Spirit. Why? Because a) Yeshua was **not physically present**; b) Yeshua was not providing them with **irrefutable evidence of His Messiahship;** c) they were not **Israel's leaders** accusing Yeshua of being **demon possessed.** All manner of every other form of sin committed, shall we say for example, by the Ninevites, as mentioned by Yeshua (or sins committed by you and me), however heinous **cannot possibly include the wilful rejection of Messiah in these unique circumstances.**

So, to be clear, we are in a position to say with confidence that the blasphemy of the Holy Spirit is this:

> **The rejection of Yeshua's Messiahship, on the grounds of demon-possession, by the Jewish leadership during the time He was physically present.**

And so to the third element, referred to as "**thinking out-of-the-box.**" In using this phrase, I really refer to the ability which Jewish believers in Christ tend to have to just seek out what the Scripture says, resisting temptations (brought to bear by the traditions of the contemporary church) to avoid what the plain meaning of the text is trying to say. The blasphemy against the Holy Spirit is an excellent example of this as, regarding sin, we tend to think that all sin is repeatable through the ages. (Think of the Ten Commandments, for instance.) This has been the problem with all those concerned about whether or not they have committed this sin. But, as Dr Fruchtenbaum's understanding states, this is (or rather *was*) a unique, **NON-REPEATABLE** sin limited in time and space which is simply not possible to commit now.[55] So, if you are one of those people beating themselves up over this issue, you can rest easy!

But! Although this is the end of our personal anxiety, it was certainly not the end of this episode's effect which was absolutely massive, shaping the following 2000 years of Jewish history by setting in motion a train of events which included the destruction of the Temple in AD 70, and the dissolution of the nation of Israel resulting in the Jewish people's subsequent dispersal and perpetual vulnerability, culminating in the infamous horror of the holocaust followed by the miraculous reinstatement of Israel as a nation and the re-gathering of its native people. (*Note: this is not to imply that the holocaust was a **direct** result of the rejection of Yeshua but that had He been accepted, the dispersion would not have occurred. The prophecies foretelling His rejection are statements of what **would** happen, not what **had** to happen.*)

Having answered our basic question "What actually is the sin?" Dr Fruchtenbaum points out that the whole Gospel narrative actually *hinges around this point*. He maintains that from the point at which the blasphemy was

---

55 Ibid.

135

committed, the Kingdom of God, which had hitherto been on offer, was in fact then **withdrawn from the nation of Israel.**[56] Compare Yeshua's benevolent words in Luke 12 earlier in His ministry:

> *"Do not be afraid, little flock, for your Father has been **pleased to give you** the kingdom"...*

... with those spoken with regard to the blasphemy issue in Matthew 12...

> *"A wicked and adulterous generation asks for a sign but none will be given it."*

Notice the massive reversal of attitude:

> *"Little flock"* becomes *"A wicked and adulterous generation";*

> *"Pleased to give you"* becomes *"none will be given it."*

People may fair-mindedly complain that it was *the leadership* who were rejecting Yeshua's Messiahship, not the everyday folk.

Two points can be made regarding this observation. First, historically, Jewish people have suffered from what Dr Fructenbaum calls the *"leadership complex"* where individuals put huge store by what their leaders say and are hugely influenced by them.[57] Second, the Hebrew Scriptures are peppered with examples of individuals and the nation of Israel suffering as a result of sinful actions committed by their leaders. This is what some Jewish believers (like Tom Bradford of *TorahClass.com*) call a *"God principle."*[58] In this

---

56 Ibid.
57 Ibid.
58 Tom Bradford, "Old Testament Studies, Deuteronomy, Lesson 3, chapters 1 and 2," *TorahClass.com*, http://www.torahclass. com/teacher/38-old-testament-studies/old-testament-

particular case, the principle is that when leaders scuff up, the rest of us suffer! Naturally, this is not something we like to acknowledge but it is there in Scripture for sure.

Dr Fruchtenbaum makes the acutely observed point that following the blasphemy which provoked Yeshua's revocation of the Kingdom, appeals for help **on the specific grounds that He was The Son of David**—a **Messianic** title—were actually rejected because He had withdrawn His offer to them **as Messiah**.[59] However, He was still willing to provide healing based simply on **personal need**. The Canaanite woman of Matthew 15:21-28 is the key example of this:

> *Leaving that place, Jesus withdrew to the region of Tyre and Sidon. A Canaanite woman from that vicinity came to him, crying out, "Lord,* **Son of David,** *have mercy on me! My daughter is demon-possessed and suffering terribly."*
>
> **Jesus did not answer a word.** *So his disciples came to him and urged him, "Send her away, for she keeps crying out after us."*
>
> *He answered, "I was sent only to the lost sheep of Israel."*

Notice that, by omitting the title, "**Son of David'**, she now rephrases her plea from one based on Yeshua being **the Messiah** to one based simply on **personal need** thus:

> *The woman came and knelt before him. "***Lord, help me!***" she said.*

Still more resistance from Yeshua...

> *He replied, "It is not right to take the children's bread and toss it to the dogs."*

studies-deuteronomy/234-lesson-3-chapter-1-and-2
59 Fruchtenbaum, "The Three Messianic Miracles," *Messianic Bible Study #035.*

By dropping the Messianic title ("*Son of David*"), she is over the first hurdle but Yeshua counters with another obstacle based on the ethnic priority—that the best "food" is reserved for Jews.

> "*Yes it is, Lord,*" *she said.* "*Even the dogs eat the crumbs that fall from their master's table.*" *Then Jesus said to her,* "**Woman, you have great faith!** *Your request is granted.*" *And her daughter was healed at that moment.*

So the woman's request was granted, *not* on the grounds of *Yeshua's Messiahship*, but because of her **great faith**.

No one is suggesting Yeshua was playing trivial semantic games with needy people or that the woman had a "light-bulb moment" and hastily dropped her use of the phrase "*Son of David.*" It is even possible that she carried on using it, but Matthew either intentionally or unintentionally structured His narrative in this way as prompted by the Holy Spirit. The possibility that Matthew may have been aware of the particular interpretation discussed here is supported by the fact that a major theme of Matthew's Gospel is indeed the *Messiahship* of Yeshua.

Becoming aware of a certain phenomenon enables us to "see" the same principle in other cases even when the application of that principle is much more subtly nuanced such as the two blind men incident in Matthew 20:29-34:

> *As Jesus and his disciples were leaving Jericho, a large crowd followed him. Two blind men were sitting by the roadside, and when they heard that Jesus was passing by, they shouted,* "*Lord,* **Son of David,** *have mercy on us!*"

*The crowd rebuked them and told them to be quiet, but they shouted all the louder, "Lord, **Son of David,** have mercy on us!"*

It is not clear whether Yeshua ignored or simply did not hear them. Either way, they had to persist with their plea...

*Jesus stopped and called them. "What do you want me to do for you?" he asked.*
***Lord,"*** *they answered, **"we want our sight.'***
*Jesus had compassion on them and touched their eyes. Immediately they received their sight and followed him.*

Notice that although the men appeared to elicit a response from Yeshua by using the title *Son of David,* Yeshua did not seek them out and they had to do a lot of shouting and attention-grabbing to, as it were, get Him to interrupt His direction of travel. (In fact, each Gospel writer records that He ***stood still,*** by implication, ***with His back towards them*** and that He did not go to *them*). Yeshua subtly shifted the frame of reference by asking their personal need. There follows a rephrased request which ***excluded*** the "Son of David" title: ***Lord,"*** *they answered, **"we want our sight."*** And it was on the compassionate grounds of personal need that the request was granted. Again, whatever the blind men and the Gospel author were or were not aware of, the fact remains that the only two occasions when Yeshua ignored people before healing them both coincided with the use and subsequent retraction of the phrase *"Son of David"*...and as good Bible "detectives," this should at least be food for thought.

139

Of course, the ideal way of establishing the degree of importance of the blasphemy issue would be, if it were otherwise possible, to ask the author, Matthew, himself... and since he was the Author's author, that, we could agree, should clinch it. However, Matthew has in indeed "arranged" for us a way of doing this which, fortunately, does not involve going to heaven to meet him. This help comes from a completely different direction: Matthew's love of literary devices, and in particular — *chiasms*.

(If the reader is not familiar with this term, there is a brief explanation in this book's final chapter so it may be advisable to read this first.)

It is generally agreed that, as well as using smaller chiasms within his Gospel, Matthew did actually structure his entire book into one epic chiasm. This is commonly depicted as follows:

A. Genealogy (past) (1:1-17)

  B. First Mary and Yeshua's birth (1:18-25)

  C. Gifts of wealth at birth (2:1-12)

  D. "Descent" into Egypt; murder of children (2:13-21)

  E. Judea avoided (2:22-23)

  F. Baptism of Yeshua (3:1–8:23)

  G. Crossing the sea (8:24–11:1)

  H. John's ministry (11:2-19)

  I. Rejection of Yeshua (11:20-24)

  J. Gifts for the new children (11:25-30)

  K. Attack of Pharisees (12:1-13)

  **L. Pharisees decide to kill the innocent Servant (12:14-21)**

  K' Condemnation of Pharisees (12:22-45)

  J' Gifts for the new children (13:1-52)

  I' Rejection of Yeshua (13:53-58)

  H' John's death (14:1-12)

  G' Crossing the sea (14:13–16:12)

  F' Transfiguration of Yeshua,(16:13–18:35)

  E' Judean ministry (19:1–20:34)

  D' "Ascent" into Jerusalem; judgment on Jews (21:1–27:56)

C' Gift of wealth at death (27:57-66)

B' Last Mary and Yeshua's resurrection (28:1-15)

A' Commission (future) (28:16-20)

Before continuing, let us take a moment to admire the exquisite symmetry in these pairings such as **A** and **A'**. The *genealogy* (physical offspring), begins with the *past* and works forwards to the *present*, whilst the *commission* (spiritual offspring) works from the *present* to the *future*.

141

Similarly elegant is the near perfect inversion (matching with "opposites") of **D** with **D'** made explicit below:

---

**D.** The **descent** into Egypt (*Gentile*)...and death of Jews... (*innocent children*)

⇓　　　⇓　　　　　⇓　⇓

**D'** The **Ascent** into Jerusalem (*Jewish*)...and judgment on Jews (*guilty leaders*)

---

Returning to the main point about the blasphemy issue, notice that this occurs in K', which, under this chiastic construction, is slightly off-centre and therefore, apparently, would not support the assertion that this was a pivotal turning point in Matthew's Gospel as far as Israel's future was and is concerned. However, what makes chiasms intriguing and "fun" is their lack of absolute definition, inviting the reader to play around and experiment with where breaks in the text should come so as to create a chiasm. That Matthew organised the text into a chiasm is not generally disputed but there is no way of knowing whether we have identified all of these pairings absolutely "correctly" as Matthew intended. Indeed, following a careful read through of the whole of Matthew's 12th chapter, I see a plausible restructuring around K through to K' may be justified and perhaps actually preferred.

The problem with the "official" chiasm is that the center sections do not correlate to the natural and therefore, obvious changes in the themes of the text. This is the same effect as pasting a number of paragraphs together, only to then re-cut them in different places. For instance, in the original, the center, "L" takes its name after a single reference in verse 14 regarding the Pharisees' desire to kill Yeshua. But in context, this is really the climax to the previous section of attacks by the Pharisees and so is better suited to that (previous) passage. In contrast, the tone of the following passage is completely different, being much gentler and softer. It is just like the way people talk when discussing someone they don't like, and then suddenly changing the subject to someone they really do! To begin such a passage with a wicked murder conspiracy surely seems totally incongruous.

In fact, as I read through Matthew 12 from the KJV, I independently "chunked" the text according to the natural changes of theme; after subsequently checking these against the NIV, I noticed that my decisions almost mirrored the sub-headings used by that translation. So, my re-jigged version of the "official" center section is as follows:

**K**. The Pharisees attack Yeshua (12:1-14)
   **L**. The characteristics of Yeshua (the good servant) (12:15-21)
      **M. The blasphemy of the Holy Spirit (**12:22-32)
   **L'** The characteristics of the Pharisees (evil vipers) (12:33-37)
**K'** Yeshua condemns the Pharisees (12:38-45)

Being careful to let the text interpret itself (rather than trying to make the text fit the thesis), this reorganization does now imbue the blasphemy issue with the pivotal importance suggested by Arnold Fruchtenbaum.

Moreover, not only can chiasms support the importance of this blasphemy issue, but this literary tool may also corroborate the actual *identity* of what it means to

143

blaspheme against the Holy Spirit as presented in this chapter. Although we have already established this, final verification may come from a particular, smaller chiasm found "hidden," Russian doll-style, inside the "M" section— the very center of the center of Matthew's Gospel. This chiasm is best presented, not using invented subheadings, but rather, by keeping to the actual Scriptures as follows:

A. *"...the son of David."* (12:22-23)

    B. *"It is only by Beelzebul, the prince of demons, that this fellow drives out demons."* (12:24)

        C. *"If Satan drives out Satan, he is divided against himself"* (12:26)

          D. *"If I drive out demons by Beelzebul..."* (12:27)

          D' *"...but if it is by the Spirit of God that I drive out demons..."* (12:28)

        C' *"...how can anyone enter a strong man's house and steal his property, unless he first ties up the strong man?"* (12:29)

    B' *"...blasphemy against the Spirit will not be forgiven."* (12:31)

A' *"...the Son of Man..."* (12:32)

Notice that as we track backwards from B' across to B, the relationship between them becomes so visible as to appear almost a *fait accompli*. B tells us what the blasphemy against the Holy Spirit is, whilst B' tells us what it is called. In chiasms, the partnered sections often represent some kind of intensification of the content found in the initial section. For example, B contains a statement which, although strong, is trumped by the catastrophic corollary result in B'. Similarly, D refers to the flawed logic of the Pharisees in contrast to D' which corrects it with the truth. C is a position of failure, whereas, C' explains the formula for success.

In many ways, our preoccupation with understanding the nature of what became known as the "unforgivable or unpardonable sin" has been a purely self-centred one, driven by our anxiety at the thought of bearing existential consequences of personal, un-forgiven sin. However, this has prevented us from investigating its actual effects on Yeshua's subsequent words and actions as well as the long-term consequences of Israel's rejection of Messiah. Regarding the theme of this book, it should be noted that these insights have come from a Jew. Could a Gentile have uncovered the truth? Very possibly—but it just seems significant that so often, the knowledge a religious Jewish person has gives them a head start on these difficult passages. So, turning to a respected Jewish believer in Yeshua for the answer makes a lot of sense.

*"And no one pours new wine into old wineskins. If he does, the new wine will burst the skins, the wine will run out and the wineskins will be ruined. No, new wine must be poured into new wineskins. And no one after drinking old wine wants the new, for he says, 'The old is better.'"*

(Luke 5:37-38)

*"A farmer went out to sow his seed. As he was scattering the seed, some fell along the path; it was trampled on, and the birds ate it up. Some fell on rocky ground, and when it came up, the plants withered because they had no moisture. Other seed fell among thorns, which grew up with it and choked the plants. Still other seed fell on good soil. It came up and yielded a crop, a hundred times more than was sown."*

(Luke 8:5-8)

# YESHUA: RECYCLER—OR *UP*CYCLER?

> Quick Summary! Most of us hold to the belief that Yeshua's words were either quotes from the Hebrew Scriptures or totally original sayings. It will surprise many that a number of parables and sayings of His were in fact similar to those known within the Jewish community of the day. This begs the question that since the Messiah obviously regarded them as worthy of use as analogies or at least allusions, then should we not likewise consider investing some study-time in investigating the Jewish culture, stories, traditions, and Rabbinic teachings whilst acknowledging that being derived from sources which lay outside of the Bible, they carry lesser validity?

## And now in more detail...

Most of us are aware that, on occasions, Yeshua quoted the Hebrew Scriptures (The Old Testament). Obviously, those who subscribe to the inspiration of the Bible as a whole have no problem with this. Thus, any words which Yeshua spoke which cannot be found elsewhere in the Scriptures we assume to be original, and this assumption is implicitly supported by His divinity. Surely His unique origins and identity must equate with unique ideas and speech? However, what is far less well known, in fact almost entirely unknown, is the surprising fact that on occasions the words, phrases, and passages spoken by Yeshua would have been *already commonly known and recognised by His Jewish listeners,* albeit in either a different or somewhat re-jigged form. One of the reasons we hang onto the belief that everything He said was new is that we constantly feel the need to protect the divine origins, integrity, and "specialness" of His words and that consequently, any hint of unoriginality might lend a certain degree of "second-handness" and downgrading to what we see as stand-alone, pristine Truth, thus depriving it of some of its glory and gravitas, which is definitely not our intent at all. (See the last chapter, *"A Word about Jewish Sources."*)

Using material, possibly already well known (in some form) by His audiences had huge benefits in enabling Yeshua to build upon a pre-established foundation of understanding. Being "primed" in the Jewish context of the day enabled His listeners to more readily receive His particular "twist" or "take" on a matter as certain phrases, idioms, and words used by Yeshua often contained "packages" of meaning or significance which His listeners could immediately "clue into." Too many of us have been almost totally unaware of this use of linguistic tradition by Yeshua, and the more one examines the Bible from a Jewish frame of reference, the more obvious it becomes just how much extra texture and richness we have denied ourselves!

For instance, Rabbi Daniel of *Jewisheyes* has written an outstanding article called *"Why did Jesus Walk on Water?"* In it, he links what Yeshua did with the crossing of the Red Sea, drawing on Jewish legends[60] which may or may not be true. Whether these legends actually happened or not is not the point since no one is claiming they are inspired Scripture. The real point is that, in the case of the example above, the disciples would have known these stories and would have related them to what they were seeing Yeshua do first hand. They would have been thinking, *This is just like Moses and the Red Sea crossing!*—just another stepping stone designed by Yeshua to bring them to the point of accepting Him as the one spoken of by Moses in Deuteronomy 18:15, *The LORD your God will raise up for you a prophet like me from among you, from your fellow Israelites. You must listen to him.*

Now read the following ancient Pharisaic proverb from the ancient Jewish source—*The Mishnah*. As you read it, see if anything sounds familiar:

Elisha ben Avuyah said: "He who studies as a child, unto what can he be compared? He can be compared to ink written upon a fresh [new] sheet of paper. But he who studies as an adult, unto what can he be compared? He can be compared to ink written on a smudged [previously used and erased] sheet of paper."

Rabbi Yose ben Yehudah of the city of Babylon said, "He who learns from the young, unto what can he be compared? He can be compared to one who

60 Rabbi Daniel Thomson, "Why did Jesus Walk on Water?" *Jewisheyes. org,* http://www.jewisheyes.org/store/

eats unripe grapes, and drinks unfermented wine from his vat. But he who learns from the old, unto what can he be compared? He can be compared to one who eats ripe grapes, and drinks old wine."

Rabbi (Meir) said: "Do not pay attention to the container but pay attention to that which is in it. **There is a new container full of old wine, and here is an old container which does not even contain new wine."** [61]

Did you guess?! Surely the last line gives it away — Luke 5:36-39 perhaps?

*He told them this parable: "No one tears a patch from a new garment and sews it on an old one. If he does, he will have torn the new garment, and the patch from the new will not match the old.*

***"And no one pours new wine into old wineskins. If he does, the new wine will burst the skins, the wine will run out and the wineskins will be ruined.***

*"No, new wine must be poured into new wineskins. And no one after drinking old wine wants the new, for he says, 'The old is better.'"*

Let us linger here for a while as this parable is almost universally misunderstood and due to the unanimity of our confidence, the true meaning in some Christian circles[62] has been kept firmly under the boot of an anti-Judaism bias.

In summary, Pastor Lancaster of *bethimmanuel.org*, a First Fruits of Zion (*ffoz.org*) writer, reminds us that to most modern evangelicals...

---

61 Mishnah: Perkei Avot (Ethics of the Fathers) 4:20.

62 A few Christian pastors teach that Yeshua is saying we must be born anew (John 3:16)—become a new creation in Messiah (2 Cor. 5:17)— before we can receive the new wine of the Holy Spirit, which is a nice teaching and rings true from a Christian perspective, but it wouldn't have been how the Jewish people of the day would've taken it.

The meaning of the parable seems obvious. The new garment is the Gospel/Grace/ Kingdom/Church and the old garment is the Old Covenant/Law/ Judaism. No one tears a new garment to patch an old one. Grace and law do not mix. Similarly, the new wine is the Gospel/Grace/Kingdom/Church and the old wineskin is the Old Covenant/Law/Judaism. Just as the new wine would burst the old skins and be spilled, so too the New Covenant Gospel of the Church Kingdom would be wasted if it was poured into the Old Covenant, Mosaic, legalistic religion of Judaism.

In almost unanimous consent interpreters and commentators have agreed that the old wine, old wineskins and the old coat are all symbols of Judaism and Law whereas the new wine and the new coat are symbols of Christianity and Grace. The traditional interpretation of the double parable can be summed up in one word: **incompatibility**. It is supposed to teach that the Old and the New are *incompatible,* that Judaism is incompatible with Christianity. The old is worn and obsolete. The Church must be a new and separate movement, not a patch attempting to prolong the institutions of the Old Covenant. The New Covenant has erased and replaced the Old. This meaning of the double parable seems obvious—or perhaps not....[63]

The problem with interpreting the parable as pitting the (old) Judaism against the (new) Gospel is that it is anachronistic, meaning, that the theme of incompatibility

---

63 Pastor D. Thomas Lancaster, "New Wine and Old Wineskins," *Beth Immanuel Sabbath Fellowship*, Hudson, Wisconsin, bethimmanuel.org, http://www.bethimmanuel.org/articles/new-wine-and-old-wineskins-parable-luke-536-39-re-examined

interpretation would not have made any sense at that time since, at the time of Yeshua, *there was no Christianity, church or "new religion"* for Judaism to "fall out" with, so how could His listeners have understood any kind of "system vs system" rivalry issue at that time? Also, *bethimmanuel. org* point out that...

> Critical scholarship now acknowledges that **Yeshua was not trying to start a new religion nor was his intention to dismantle Judaism.**[64]

...and Yeshua Himself said in Matthew 5:17, *"I have not come to abolish them (the law and the prophets) but to fulfil them."*...where the word "fulfil" means to bring out its most rounded and perfect rendition/interpretation, leading to its most effective, intended, practical outworking. Also, if, as the common understanding maintains, the **old** Judaism is bad then why does Yeshua end His parable by saying that those who have tried both the old and the new reckon that,*"...the old is better"*?

But, if we dispense with any unintended anti-Semitic bias we may have, by going back to the original cultural CONTEXT which, in this case is the ancient Pharisaic proverb, and *allowing the text to interpret itself* then we can see that the proverb and thus Yeshua's use of it is talking not about conflict between religious institutions but about types of *teachers, teachings and disciples.* Notice also the immediate context within the text where we find Yeshua's parable. Levi is having a banquet and the Pharisees are having a hard time understanding Yeshua's choice of disciples as they clearly did not represent the cream of what was available, which was out of character

---

64 ibid.

with the natural choices a Pharisee would normally make. We know from Acts 4 that Luke returns to this theme of the "type" of disciples they were, noting that the Pharisees considered them *ignorant and unlearned men*." The website *bethimmanuel.org* paint an amusing picture of the banquet at Levi's house:

> As the meal progresses, the Pharisees began to ask Yeshua's disciples some questions such as, "How often do you fast?" The disciples are unable to answer with their mouths full, so they shrug and look at Yeshua.[65]

Returning to the parable and the ancient proverb then, Lancaster cracks the "code" of these metaphors as follows:

- New garment = previously uneducated students
- Old garment = previously educated students
- Patch = teaching
- New wineskins = previously uneducated students
- Old wineskins = previously educated students
- New wine = new teaching
- Old wine = previous teaching
- Singular Meaning = New teaching requires previously uneducated students in order to be received.[66]

So, with this de-coding in mind, this ffoz.org writer has paraphrased Yeshua's double parable. (I have made some changes in brackets to add clarity.)

> No one takes a lesson meant for a new [impressionable] student and tries to teach it to an old (already educated) student (who has their own ideas). If he does, he will fail to teach the new

---

65 Ibid.
66 Ibid.

student, and the lesson meant for the new student will be rejected by the old student anyway—so there is no net benefit to anyone.

No one teaches new interpretations about Torah to old (previously educated) students [who are already locked into their own ideas]. If he does, the new teaching will be rejected and the student will be lost [become confused]. [Still no benefit!] No. Instead new Torah-teaching must be taught to new students. And no one after having received old teaching (previous education) wants the new, for he says, "The old teaching [what he is comfortable with] is better." [67]

In short, the parable's message is...

**YOU CAN'T TEACH AN OLD DOG NEW TRICKS!**

...combined with...

**I'D RATHER TEACH A SIMPLE MAN WHO KNOWS NOTHING THAN AN EDUCATED MAN WHO THINKS HE KNOWS EVERYTHING!**

So there we have it—mission accomplished! By sitting under Torah-teachers like Rabbi Daniel Thomson and other sources, and by referring back to the original parable as already fully incorporated into Jewish oral culture, we can cross-check them with our understanding of these Bible passages—and not just those we consider "tricky" since even when we feel sure about a particular passage such as the one just discussed, our very confidence is likely to create a false sense of security. This can lead (ironically like the new teaching/old disciple model) to a lack of motivation to explore different possible interpretations.

---

67 Ibid.

The "new" teaching Yeshua was "getting at" was His particular "take" on the Mosaic Law/Instruction—in short, the proper meanings of the Torah as originally intended by God Himself.

And finally, have a look at this one taken from *The Mishnah*, which is a section devoted to ethics and moral wisdom:

> There are four (disciples) who sit before the wise (teachers): a sponge, a funnel, a strainer and a sieve. The sponge soaks up everything. The funnel takes in at one end and lets out at the other. The strainer lets out the wine and keeps the dregs. The sieve lets out the meal and keeps the fine flour.[68]

So we have here four types of disciples of varying characteristics with the proverb ending with the best one, the "sieve." Which parable told by Yeshua features four types of learner, has the same structure as this ancient proverb and ends with the most commendable learner? It can only be The Parable of the Sower—or as some would say, the Parable of the Soils.

> *A farmer went out to sow his seed. As he was scattering the seed, some fell along the path; it was trampled on, and the birds ate it up. Some fell on rocky ground, and when it came up, the plants withered because they had no moisture. Other seed fell among thorns, which grew up with it and choked the plants. Still other seed fell on good soil. It came up and yielded a crop, a hundred times more than was sown."* ~ Luke 8:5-8

---

68 *Mishna:* Pirkei Avot (Ethics of the Fathers) 5:15-18, http://www.sefaria. org/Pirkei_Avot.5.15-18?lang=en&layout=lines&sidebarLang=all

That is not to say that Yeshua perfectly reproduces this proverb because He does not, but rather He modifies it to give it His own preferred emphasis which is spiritual *profit and reproduction* (the crop produced after its own kind).

With the help of Rabbi Daniel Thomson's comments, I have arranged the comparison between the proverb and Yeshua's own parable to clarify the similarities:

| Disciple metaphor from the proverb | Is this a preferred type of learner? | Rabbi Daniel Thomson's comments about the proverb's metaphors for the types of disciples. | Links with Yeshua's parable of the sower |
|---|---|---|---|
| The sponge | NO | This disciple soaks everything up. Isn't that what we want though? No, because they soak up good and bad teaching—lots of enthusiasm but no discernment. | The thorny ground—The good results get mixed up with the bad which ultimately dominate the good |
| The funnel | NO | This disciple takes it all in, retains it for a short while but then failing to hold on to it— possibly when the going gets tough—lets it all go. | The rocky soil—The seed maintains growth for a while but has no root so it comes to nothing. |
| The strainer | NO | This disciple retains bad teaching but not the good so is a non-starter. | The path where the seed is trampled and eaten immediately. |
| The sieve | YES | This disciple knows the good teaching when they see it but also knows how to separate it from any bad. | The good soil which maintains growth long enough to produce a crop. |

The main difference between the proverb and Yeshua's parable is that whilst both are concerned with the types of disciple, Yeshua refers to the consequential outcome of the fruitful disciple which is **reproduction.**

Daniel Thomson draws out a helpful application from the "sieve" metaphor. He says that in a perfect world we should not be subject to bad teaching but that, on occasions, we may encounter a teaching, the content of which is valid but the manner in which it may have been presented offends us. This could be a personal criticism which we reject simply because we take offense at the way it was said, or the person's approach or even appearance may all conspire to "rub us up the wrong way." The "sieve" disciple and the "good soil" will have the maturity to sift the content from the manner, so-to-speak, and learn their lesson despite any off-putting, cosmetic irritations.

The fact that Yeshua used *four* types of soil in His parable would also have come as no surprise to His audience. A cursory examination of the section of text either side of where the proverb is found (Avot 5:13-18) makes it abundantly clear as to why Yeshua chose four disciple types in His parable since the number "four" is so prevalent. There are mentioned:

*Four* types of people, *four* types of temperament, *four* characteristics in student, *four* types who give charity, *four* types who go to the house of study and the proverb we have examined—the *four* types of who sit before the wise.

These examples show just how much Yeshua drew on and adapted the stories, legends, and wisdom writings from His own culture for His own purposes. The fact that we quite rightly accept Yeshua's Words as Scripture surely suggests that we would do well to familiarize ourselves with the ancient Jewish writings such as the Talmud and Mishnah since some of His teachings were contextually derived from them.

**NOTE:** Since the rabbis quoted in this chapter lived after the time of Yeshua, there are those who assert that it was *they* who copied *Him*, not the other way round. But "copying" is really not the issue here—with all its negative connotations—whichever way round it is. This is discussed more fully in the chapter called "*A Word About Jewish Sources.*"

There was a rich man who was dressed in purple and fine linen and lived in luxury every day. At his gate was laid a beggar named Lazarus, covered with sores and longing to eat what fell from the rich man's table. Even the dogs came and licked his sores.

The time came when the beggar died and the angels carried him to Abraham's side. The rich man also died and was buried. In Hades, where he was in torment, he looked up and saw Abraham far away, with Lazarus by his side. So he called to him, "Father Abraham, have pity on me and send Lazarus to dip the tip of his finger in water and cool my tongue, because I am in agony in this fire."

But Abraham replied, "Son, remember that in your lifetime you received your good things, while Lazarus received bad things, but now he is comforted here and you are in agony. And besides all this, between us and you a great chasm has been set in place, so that those who want to go from here to you cannot, nor can anyone cross over from there to us."

He answered, "Then I beg you, father, send Lazarus to my family, for I have five brothers. Let him warn them, so that they will not also come to this place of torment."

Abraham replied, "They have Moses and the Prophets; let them listen to them."

"No, father Abraham," he said, "but if someone from the dead goes to them, they will repent."

He said to him, "If they do not listen to Moses and the Prophets, they will not be convinced even if some-one rises from the dead."

(Luke 16:19-31)

# THE RICH MAN AND LAZARUS—PARABLE OR LITERAL?

Quick Summary! Some people think this story is a parable while others believe it to be literal narrative because it uses actual names which parables usually do not. However, when we closely examine both the Hebrew Scriptures and the Jewish culture of the day, we arrive at a surprising conclusion—that the story is both literal and parable. The trick is to know what the Jews of the day knew, because *they* were Yeshua's audience.

## And now in more detail...

In attempting to understand this passage, most of us initially assume it to be a parable, coming as it does, fifth in an apparent sequence of five parables, the first four being undisputed. However, after digging around a bit...and a few commentaries later, we then change our minds, the most oft cited reason being the use of specific names. The argument goes: Parables do not use actual names as they seek to teach generalised truth whereas literal narrative is effectively a recount of specific events and characters. Interestingly, Arnold Fruchtenbaum of *Ariel Ministries* subscribes to this view and, taking the passage as literal, he integrates it into extremely coherent description and explanation of the Hebrew idea known as *Sheol* which may well prove consistent and compelling in tying together numerous Scripture references regarding the place where Old Testament souls resided following death.[69] However, after reading a compelling article by J. Preston Eby who has examined this passage in great detail,[70] I find myself falling back into the "parable" camp.

The complicating factor is the fact that, in my opinion, J. Preston Eby is correct in his assertion that this passage is indeed a parable but that the difficulties he has in accepting the literal reality of "Abraham's bosom" are actually unnecessary if we bring into play Arnold Fruchtenbaum's illuminating presentation of Sheol.

Therefore, what follows is a synopsis of Eby's article with Fruchtenbaum's explanation of Sheol/Abraham's bosom introduced at the appropriate point to help resolve Eby's difficulties. The desired effect will be a more coherent and rounded appreciation of an incredibly misunderstood passage—hopefully!

Eby begins by pointing out, quite rightly, that, as always, **CONTEXT is KING!** And the context here is that Yeshua's "real time" audience was a mixture of "tax collectors and

69 Arnold Fruchtenbaum, PhD., "The Place of the Dead," *Messianic Bible Study 107,* ariel.org, http://www.arielm.org/dcs/pdf/mbs107m.pdf, pp. 18-19.
70 J. Preston Eby, "Abraham's Bosom," *The Pathfinder,* Godfire.net, https://www.godfire.net/eby/abrahams.html

sinners" mingled with Pharisees as specified at the start of Luke chapter 15. In this setting, Yeshua begins his five stories with Luke's introduction, *"Then Jesus told them this parable"* (NIV). Eby maintains that the Greek here is emphatic and literally reads, *"the* parable this," strongly implying that the subsequent five stories are *all* parables and should be viewed as a *single cluster*. The chapter break at chapter 16 unnaturally splits the sequence of stories but this red herring can be ignored as the original text of course had no chapter or verse divisions. Although the five stories then are a "package," we notice that the first three are given as *encouragement* for the "tax collectors and sinners" section of his audience whilst the last two served as *condemnation* for the self-righteous Pharisees.

So, who is the rich man anyway? Eby makes the point that there is no reason to think that this character represents *all* lost sinners; no such negative link is made between the man's material and spiritual state. The simplistic formula: "Rich = lost/ Poor = saved" is not supported by the text. However, even in hell, the rich man cried out *"FATHER! Abraham,"* identifying himself as a member of the elect—the Jewish nation; and when Abraham addresses the rich man, he confirms his identity by answering *"Son."* Moreover, the man is *"...clothed in **purple** and fine linen"* and fared *"... sumptuously every day...."* Considering Yeshua's audience and the reference to the colour purple, the rich man can be taken as representing **the tribe of Judah**—the royal tribe from which Jewish kings originated, and in particular, the Pharisees who personified Judah's spiritual leadership. Now

163

look at the word translated as *"you"* in English. The actual Greek word is very revealing when translated literally and changes this...

> So he called to him, "Father Abraham, have pity on me and send Lazarus to dip the tip of his finger in water and cool my tongue, because I am in agony in this fire."
>
> But Abraham replied, "Son, remember that in your lifetime you received your good things, while Lazarus received bad things, but now he is comforted here and you are in agony. And besides all this, between us and you a great chasm has been set in place, so that those who want to go from here to you cannot, nor can anyone cross over from there to us."          ~ Luke 16:24-26

...to this...

> So he called to him, "Father Abraham, have pity on me and send Lazarus to dip the tip of his finger in water and cool my tongue, because I am in agony in this fire."
>
> But Abraham replied, "Son, remember that in your lifetime you received your good things, while Lazarus received bad things, but now he is comforted here and you are in agony. And besides all this, between us and **YOU PEOPLE** a great chasm has been set in place, so that **THE ONES** who want to go from here to **YOU PEOPLE** cannot, nor can anyone cross over from there to us."

Clearly then, the rich man represents a *collective* group of people, not an *individual*. To describe the many ways in which the man was rich, I have reproduced a section from Eby's article below:

> This rich man "fared sumptuously every day." But this is not talking about natural food. The

Jewish nation was the favourite of heaven—rich in the mercies and blessings of the Lord. No nation in the history of time had been so highly favoured as the house of Judah. They had the elaborate sacrificial service of the great and glorious temple in Jerusalem. They had the Scriptures, the holy law and covenant of Yahweh. They had the oracles of God, the prophets. They were rich in covenants and promises, rich in the word of God that had been delivered to them. Judah was, indeed, a RICH MAN—with the very riches from the hand of God—rich in oil and wine, rich in doctrine, rich in word, rich in history of holy men, rich in ritual and pomp and ceremony. Ah—how rich he was! Paul spoke exultantly of this vast wealth possessed by Judah, saying, *"For I could wish that myself were accursed from Christ for my brothers, my kinsmen according to the flesh: who are Israelites; to whom pertains the adoption, and the glory, and the covenants, and the giving of the law, and the service of God, and the promises; whose are the fathers, and of whom as concerning the flesh Christ came, who is over all, God blessed for ever"* (Rom. 9:3-5).[71]

Yes! He was rich indeed!

So, having established the rich man's nationality as Jewish, there is a final clue which reinforces his ethnic identity as being representative of Judah. The rich man pleads with Abraham to send Lazarus to his father's house to warn his **five brethren** *"lest they also come into this place of torment."* Has the number five been randomly selected? Unlikely. Anyone aware of Jewish numerology should instinctively be alerted to the possibility of significance

71 Ibid (J. Preston Eby).

here. So the question is, in the context of what we already know about the rich man, is there a "five" which has a direct connection to the rich man's identity. Eby points out that...

> ... The rich man is a son of ABRAHAM, through Isaac and Jacob, and you have only to read through the lists of the offspring of Abraham to find out who it was that had five brethren. [72]

> *Now the sons of Jacob were twelve: the sons of Leah; Reuben, Jacob's first born, and Simeon, and Levi, and Judah, and Issachar, and Zebulun: the sons of Rachel; Joseph, and Benjamin: and the sons of Bilhah, Rachel's handmaid; Dan, and Naphtali: and the sons of Zilpah, Leah's handmaid; Gad, and Asher: these are the sons of Jacob, which were born to him in Padan-aram"*
> ~ Gen. 35:22-26

This passage plainly reveals that **JUDAH had five brethren.** Jacob's first wife was Leah, and of Leah were born **Reuben, Simeon, Levi, Judah, Issachar, and Zebulun.** These were all full-blood brothers. Judah was one of Leah's six sons. He had five brethren! **So when this rich man says, "I have five brethren," it confirms his identity!**[73]

The Pharisees, no doubt already offended by their suspicions that Yeshua was addressing them, must have been outraged that He was publicly announcing their eternal damnation; all the more since Jews considered their descent from Abraham alone to be sufficient to secure God's welcome into some form of eternal Paradise.

---

72 Ibid.
73 Ibid.

So there we have it—the rich man represents the southern kingdom of the royal tribe of Judah!

Now to the identity of Lazarus. The key factor here hinges on the phrase *"Even (or moreover) the dogs..."* Eby's colleague and friend Elwin Roach ran some exhaustive research into the Greek in this passage and found that the word which comes over to us as *"moreover"* is in fact better and more literally translated as *"the other things"* or in this case, *"the other dogs."* Eby devotes a substantial paragraph detailing the grammatical reasoning for this but, cutting to the chase, the obvious implication is that **LAZARUS IS JUST AS MUCH A DOG AS THE ONES LICKING HIS SORES.** So, figuratively speaking, who are these dogs?

Rabbi Daniel Thomson of *Jewisheyes* points out that Jews frequently refer to people groups by metaphorical pseudonyms.[74] Broadly speaking, the heathen, non-Jewish nations were referred to as dogs but not in the sense that we understand the term. Calling someone a dog in western culture is assumed to be pejorative, often conveyed with a derogatory snarl or sneer. In Jewish culture however, the term alluded to the surrounding nations' need of the Jews who held sole rights to all of covenants and blessings of God. True it is that dogs were unclean animals but uncleanness is more of a ceremonial state than a moral statement. Thus, it was right for the "dogs" to be fed, but not "sumptuously" as the rich man (Judah) was, due to his privileged position in God's eyes.

---

74 Rabbi Daniel Thomson, "Gospels and The Acts Through Jewish Eyes," mp3 Download, No.3 Matthew 5-7, *Jewisheyes.org*

Interestingly, we see these pseudonyms used in the story of the Syrophoenician woman. When Yeshua told her that *"It is not right to throw the children's bread to the **dogs**"* she knew exactly what he meant and far from reacting with offence, used the metaphor to her advantage: *"Yes Lord, but even the dogs eat the crumbs from their master's table."* Furthermore, there are two words in Greek for dogs and the one used here is more akin to "puppy" or "pets."

If we, as Gentiles, were looking for offense then what about the Jews? What are they known as? Sheep!—known for their need of protection, a propensity to stray blindly into danger and general lack of sense! But some Gentiles were seen as worse than others. Rome, being the Jews' oppressors were known as "swine" in the culture of the day. This is a far less flattering appellation and may stem from the fact that Romans were steeped in polytheistic idolatry making them, like pigs, not just unclean but willing to consume any trash (false god) they could find. Yeshua referred to King Herod as a fox, which we (and most Gentile commentaries) assume to mean cunning but then people in Yeshua's time were not brought up on Grimm's fairy tales. With Herod's reputation as a dangerous and unscrupulous leader in mind, Yeshua was referring to his (the fox's) unsuitability to rule the Jews (sheep).

Thus, we have a neat tying together of the Syrophoenician woman and the *"Lazarus dogs."* The former lived at the outer limit of Israel, the place of peripheral but potential blessing and was prepared to "scavenge" any crumbs which came her way; and this is in like manner to Lazarus, who sat at the city gates—at the furthest extremity—and begged for scraps.

We now reach the crux of the parable or "literal (?)" issue: It is noticeable that the four preceding parables, despite not being actual "journalistic" events, so-to-speak, we notice that all of them *actually could have been!* That is, the **CONTEXTS** are all **REAL**; there *really could* have been a *"prodigal son"* or a *"lost coin"* or a *"shrewd manager"* because the details included were viable, rational, and feasible in real life. Therefore, if Eby is convinced that *"The Rich man and Lazarus"* is a parable because the preceding sequence of four are, then might we assume that it is also set in a **REAL, AUTHENTIC CONTEXT** because all the others are too? Is it likely that Yeshua would tell entirely fantasy myths about such a solemn matter?

But what about Eby's grave (no pun intended) concerns mentioned in his original article? For instance he asks:

> Could anyone enjoy the bliss (?) of heaven while compelled to listen to the hopeless, screaming pleas of unsaved loved ones and friends just across the narrow gulf. Would not such harrowing din somewhat disturb the heavenly choir with its discord? [75]

We notice from this quote that Eby believes that Abraham's Bosom to be synonymous with Heaven, that they are one and the same place. But is this true? This is where Arnold Fruchtenbaum's exegesis on "The Place(s) of the Dead" in his masterly tome *Footsteps of the Messiah* can clear up these inconsistencies and dilemmas. To do this, a brief paraphrasing of Dr Fruchtenbaum's chapter is needed.

---

75   J. Preston Eby, "Abraham's Bosom," *The Pathfinder,* Godfire.net, https://www.godfire.net/eby/abrahams.html

Dr Fruchtenbaum states that *Sheol* (in Hebrew) and *Hades* (in Greek) are one and the same place and according to Ezekiel 26:20; 31:14; Ephesians 4:9-10 and other references, is located in the nether (or lower) parts of the earth. Further, Matthew 12:40 implies that Hades is in the *heart* or the centre of the earth.[76] Dr Fruchtenbaum maintains that...

> This is one of the reasons why Sheol or Hades is temporary, because when this earth is done away with at the end of the Messianic Kingdom [in preparation for the New Heaven and New Earth], Sheol or Hades will no longer exist.[77]

*Sheol* or *Hades* is organised in a particular way with two main compartments. One compartment contained the righteous souls who died between Adam and the ascension of Yeshua. This was known as *Abraham's Bosom* and is where *Paradise* was located. The second main compartment has two further subdivisions, one of which is subdivided again. The first subdivision (better known as Hell) contains unrighteous human souls and is also known as *Abbadon* and *The Pit*. The final two subdivisions are known as the *Abyss* which is the place of temporary confinement for fallen angels whilst the other subdivision is known as *Tartarus* which is kind of a "special case"—the place of confinement for those angels who sinned in Genesis 6. I have put together the following diagram of this, which was the situation (note) *up until the death of Yeshua.*

---

76 Arnold Fruchtenbaum, PhD., "The Place of the Dead," *Messianic Bible Study 107,* Ariel.org, http://www.arielm.org/dcs/pdf/mbs107m.pdf, p. 17.
77 Ibid., p. 17.

| 1st Compartment: | 2nd Compartment | | |
|---|---|---|---|
| Abraham's Bosom/ Paradise | Hell/ Abbadon/ The Pit | The Abyss | Tartarus |
| Souls of the Righteous | Souls of the Unrighteous | Fallen angels | Angels who sinned in Genesis 6 |

So, back to the parable, Abraham's Bosom and Heaven are not the same place. True, this does not satisfy all of Eby's concerns, such as, for instance, a mother having to view her son's suffering in the distance which would not constitute much of a "paradise." However, some latitude must be allowed for the fact that the context may well be a spiritual reality but surely, a reality which must be almost impossible to depict or convey in the ordinary language at our disposal.

To return to the diagram above, Ephesians 4:9 tells us that Yeshua *"descended into the lower parts of the earth"* where, according to 1st Peter 3:18-19, He preached to the *"spirits in prison."* The Greek for *"preach"* here really means *"make a proclamation"* and so, following His death Yeshua descended into the righteous side of Sheol from where He proclaimed that His death guaranteed the judgment on the unsaved. This concurs nicely with the parable of the Rich man and Lazarus since, in the story it was possible to communicate (but not move) across the gulf between the two compartments. It also answers the oft-asked question *"Where did the thief on the Cross go when he died?"* Dr Fruchtenbaum's explanation of the structure of Sheol or Hades enables us to answer this quite easily since Yeshua said that the man would be with him in ***paradise on***

171

*that very same day.* The three days spent in the tomb is something of a misnomer as Yeshua's *body* was indeed there as, prophetically speaking, it had to be, but his *spirit* was clearing up unfinished business in Sheol.

However, the diagram above does not represent the case now as Ephesians 4:8-10 tells us that as He ascended, He *"led captivity captive,"* or *"He led captives in His train."* Because of the unique efficacy of Yeshua's blood, the righteous believers in Sheol were set free to enter Heaven Proper since although, as Dr Fruchtenbaum puts it, "the animal sacrifices were enough to keep a person out of Hell, they were insufficient to get him/her into Heaven." [78] (We might also add that the blood of bulls and goats was also certainly not sufficient to remove the "driver" of sins—the sin nature itself, or as Jews call it, the "evil inclination"). Therefore, the way was now clear for the righteous dead to ascend into Heaven with Yeshua.

Having done His work, and having emptied the righteous side of Sheol, the need for this compartment has therefore been eliminated and Paradise is now located in Heaven—the two *do now* refer to the same place. We could refer to this as a *dynamic* model of Paradise/ Heaven since the situation changed following the death of Yeshua. The reason so many of us have been confused by this subject is that we have assumed the place of the dead to be static and unchanging. Adopting Dr Fruchtenbaum's model does resolve these difficulties.

So, the position prior to Messiah's death could be summed up as, *to be absent from the body is to be present with the*

78 Ibid., pp. 18-19.

*other righteous (not the Lord—yet!),* whereas now, there is no doubt from 2 Corinthians 5:8 and Philippians 1:21-23 that *to be absent from the body is to be present with the Lord*—it is as simple as that. And to complete the picture, some may be asking, but what about the place known as Gehenna or the Lake of Fire? Quite simply, this will be the eternal abode of those souls who currently reside in the unrighteous side of Sheol when Sheol dissolves with the introduction of the New Heaven and New Earth. Either way, Sheol was and is a *temporary* place of confinement. The next diagram clarifies the present situation and place of those who have passed away:

| Heaven (with the Lord—not Sheol) | 2$^{nd}$ Compartment (Sheol) (Awaiting judgment and eternity in the Lake of Fire—known as the "second death") | | |
|---|---|---|---|
| The Righteous (those justified by faith prior to death of Yeshua) + those justified by faith in Yeshua since His death | Hell/ Abbadon/ The Pit | The Abyss | Tartarus |
| | Souls of the Unrighteous | Fallen angels | Angels who sinned in Genesis 6 |

But what about the name "Lazarus"? If he represents the surrounding heathen nations then what is he doing with a Jewish name; is this not an inconsistency? To answer this, consider this section from Eby's article:

> Without doubt Lazarus represented the neighbour kingdoms in Asia, Africa and Europe, right at Judah's gate, without promise, without

173

covenant, without hope, without Christ, without God in the world. It is interesting to note that LAZARUS is the Greek form of the Hebrew name ELEAZAR meaning "he whom God helps," or "whom God aids." The Greek word for "name" is ONOMA, and not only means a "name," but also carries the thought of ONE POSSESSING A CERTAIN CHARACTER. Putting this all together the passage could well be translated, "There was a certain begging one who POSSESSED THE *CHARACTER OF NEEDING GOD'S AID.*" [79]

A classic Jewish device—weaving a name's inherent meaning into the text to enhance the effect.

And so, we are now in a position to say that this story may well be a parable but one which is a "special case" with its CONTEXT being unverifiable, not because we lack trust that it is indeed a REAL CONTEXT but that, dealing with the place of the deceased, it is necessarily impossible to relate it to a familiar experience.

But what is the parable saying? Yeshua is saying that the Judah/ Israel of the day were in real danger of finding themselves swapped places with the nations round about as a result of rejecting their Messiah and relying on their "righteous acts" —works and traditions; in short, trusting in the mere fact of their Jewish ethnic identity to secure their place in Abraham's Bosom.

Once again, we see Yeshua using *His* knowledge of His *audience's* knowledge for *His* own ends and this passage is a good example because in the ancient Jewish writings

---

79 J. Preston Eby, "Abraham's Bosom," *The Pathfinder,* Godfire.net, https:// www.godfire.net/eby/abrahams.html

(*Bereshit Rabbah 48a*) we find a clue as to why Yeshua included Abraham in his story:

> Rabbi Levi said: "In the hereafter, Avraham [Abraham] will sit at the entrance to Gehenna [the bad side of Sheol] and permit no uncircumcised Israelite to descend therein.[80]

So the understanding prevalent at that time was that an Israelite's salvation was merely dependent upon physical circumcision which Yeshua turned on its head by putting the "dogs" (*spiritual* Israelites) in "Abraham's bosom" and the "rich man" (the *physical* Israelites) beyond help. This severed the simple but false belief that physical lineage and circumcision equaled automatic salvation.

However, we also know that Romans 4:3 says:

> *What does Scripture say? "Abraham **believed** God, and **it was credited to him** as righteousness."*

It was faith in God's promises which put Abraham into the "righteous" side of Sheol and although not a natural heir to the same promises, Lazarus was there too as his faith figuratively expressed in his willingness to scavenge at the city gates was acceptable to God as the Hebrew Scriptures tell us that *Abraham would be a father of **many (non-Jewish) nations**.*

Like the Syrophonecian woman, the heathen nations (Lazarus) were capable of expressing faith in Messiah and trust in Him driven by their need. Both had faith that, in

---

80 Genesis Rabbah, Vayera 48:8, p. 409 in the online English translation at Archive.org/stream/RabbaGenesis, https://archive.org/stream/RabbaGenesis/midrashrabbahgen027557mbp#page/n455/mode/2up

their spiritual hunger, even the scraps from the master's table would be sufficient for their needs in contradistinction to Israel's leaders who, for all their sumptuous inheritance of covenantal promises and blessings were heading towards rejection by God and eternal destruction due to their blind refusal to recognise the time of God's coming to them in Messiah Yeshua.

Of course, this is prophetic and continues to be fulfilled today. Since the rejection of Yeshua by the Jerusalem authorities—prolonging the abuse and suffering of the Jewish people at the hands of a hostile Gentile-dominated world for at least 2000 years—God, in His genius has used the interim time span to offer Himself to "Lazarus" —the Gentile nations who have indeed been responsive. The problem we Gentiles have is that this reversal of spiritual fortunes has "gone to our heads" so-to-speak, and far too many of us have arrogated to ourselves a mandate to write the Jews off on God's behalf, cutting them out of their own "olive tree."

However, as Paul says in Romans, when the number of Gentiles is complete, Messiah Yeshua will reoffer Himself to "the rich man"—Judah/ The Jewish people but this time they will, without exception, say YES! ...and *"all Israel will be saved"*—a happy ending indeed!

# APPENDIX

# CHIASMS

In the chapter, *"Unforgivably Unrepeatable"* in this book, reference is made to **chiasms**, a literary method which many Bible authors used for organising their texts. To our great loss, chiasms have been almost entirely overlooked by most Bible teachers despite the fact that no one doubts their existence within the text of Scripture. The best way to understand and appreciate this clever and numinous literary device used by so many Bible authors is to demonstrate a simple one, such as that found in Matthew 6. The text's "visible" organisation is the one we are all familiar with:

*"No one can serve two masters. Either you will hate the one and love the other, or you will be devoted to the one and despise the other. You cannot serve both God and money."*

From a cursory scan of this text, the main point seems obvious to the Western observer. Having been trained (by our academic or cultural background), to find the main theme of any paragraph usually, either at its beginning or end (but **rarely in the middle,** note), we may swiftly conclude that Yeshua is saying that you have a choice: to serve either God or money—but not both. Whilst this conclusion is good and undoubtedly germane to the intended theme, if we were to rearrange the text with due regard to how the words relate to each other then an equally, if not even more profound, meaning emerges. The rearrangement needed is a *chiastic* one and can be seen as follows:

**A**... *"No one can serve two masters.*

  **B**...*Either you will hate the one*

   **C**...*and love the other,*

   **C'**...*or you will be devoted to one*

  **B'**...*and despise the other.*

**A'**...*You cannot serve God and money."*

When the text is rearranged like this (often described as half an "X"), the thematic similarity (often called "*symmetry*") between A and A'...and B and B' provides the evidence that this section of the text was indeed, intentionally written as a chiasm. A with A' cover the theme of not serving two masters whilst the theme of B with B' covers the result if you do. Understandably then, the A with A' theme appears unequivocally to be Matthew's main message. However, it is generally believed that, with regard to chiasms, the author's intended theme and message actually lie, not at the beginning or the end but *in the middle*—known as the *centre-point*.

In chiasms, there is often only one central phrase but in our example above, there are two: C with C'. This has caused some commentators to re-evaluate what the text is really trying to say which is, that you may indeed be serving

God and not money, but even more important is to *love* God from which your ***devotional service*** will flow since it is possible to serve God *without* loving Him—and some do!

Chiasms are often used by secular communicators as an aide memoir, even though the user may not even have heard of the term. Take this very short admonition for example: *"Don't get fit to run. Run to get fit!"* Surely the message here is obvious—and it is, but where is the *emphasis*? Rearranging the clauses into a chiastic structure, we get the following:

> A...Don't get fit...
>
> B... to run
>
> **B'**...Run
>
> **A'**...to get fit!

We may have assumed that the intended theme here is "getting fit." However, when viewed "chiastically," the central emphasis is actually on "**RUN!**'...Why? Because if you do, the fitness will look after itself.

There are literally hundreds of chiasms in the Bible. Sometimes, they can overlap with other chiasms or, like the example in the chapter, *"Unforgivably Unrepeatable,"* can actually be found "stacked" inside a larger one. Their contribution to our study of Bible passages is that, unlike the usual approach where we are commonly encouraged to derive our own, personal meanings and themes, chiasms invite us to discover what the *actual author's* and therefore *God's* central messages are.

Why not find a passage you are familiar with, which is also written as a chiasm (the internet is the obvious place to go[81] [82]) and try reading it, so-to-speak, from the "edges" inwards, towards the centre-point? It will offer you a novel and unique perspective on a passage you thought you knew! When I have done this, it is remarkable how my memory has fastened onto and retained the centre-point of a passage. Not only so, but the paired links between the sections will also add to your appreciation of the Bible's structural integrity; like the floor joists of a house which span the internal space to connect two walls, the whole entity is designed for support, unity and purpose.

---

81 Lee Anderson Jr., "A Deeper Understanding of the Flood—Making the Most of the Message," at *Answersingenesis.org*, April 1, 2014, is an excellent place to start. https://answersingenesis.org/the-flood/making-the-most-of-the-message/

82 Also, try doing an image search for *Noah's chiasm* for a very visual demonstration of the chiastic structure.

# A WORD ABOUT JEWISH SOURCES

In this book, reference is made to various ancient Jewish documents and sources. A brief explanation of these will help the reader understand the nature of these sources and why they have been used in this book, especially in the chapter, *"Yeshua: Recycler or Upcycler?"*

As soon as the Torah, the Written Law, was given on Mount Sinai, Moses and the Priests and Levites that God set up as judges had to interpret the law to apply it to individual cases, as we see Moses doing before Torah in Exodus 18. These interpretations were not written down, but instead were passed along in oral teachings as the *Oral Law*. Orthodox Judaism believes the Oral Law was given by God along with the Written Law. Originally, in their minds, these two elements were seen as complimentary; as DNA has to decode its own code, so was the oral law to the Written.

As these statutes were passed on and amplified, concerns began to grow that, with the passing of time and persecution, these oral traditions could become forgotten and lost forever, especially after the Temple was destroyed by the Romans. These concerns prompted a scholarly rabbi called *Yehuda NaNasi* (~135-217 AD) to compile these traditions into a compendium which became known as the **Mishnah** (meaning *'To study and review'*). This was completed around 200 AD. A key feature and achievement of the Mishnah was that, for the first time, these traditions were now collated and **organized**, specifically into six "orders," each covering a different aspect of daily life. For example, the "order" called *Nashim* (Women) covers issues of marriage and divorce.

Consistent with that great aphorism, *"Two Jews – three opinions,"* inevitably, the Mishnah itself was then analyzed and commented upon, resulting in what is known as the **Gemara**. Put the Mishnah and Gemara together, and you have what is called (confusingly), the **Talmud**. The more well-known version of the Gemara is called the **Babylonian Talmud** as it was published in Babylonia.

When you read the Talmud, you read an awful lot of arguments! It seems to us that the rabbis just cannot stop splitting hairs, whereas, in actual fact, this kind of debate (known as *pilput*) is an abstract way of distilling the essence of a Torah principle. A perfume manufacturer may go to great lengths to extract only a single drop of a flower's aromatic chemical, which will then represent that flower's irreducible essence. In the same way, rarely will you find a rabbi disputing a *major* principle (for instance, whether the Sabbath should be observed or not), but we may find them debating a certain *detail* pertaining to Sabbath observance in order to seek out that detail's underlying meanings and purposes.

The concept of "oral teachings" was especially relevant when the Jews were exiled to Babylon and found themselves with no land, no Temple and therefore, no sacrificial system. Clearly, they faced the "real-time" and unique challenge of working out how to live God's Torah in a completely new and alien situation. Naturally, this led to dramatic changes in Jewish religious life. (This was when the idea of having their lives centred around synagogues was developed.) With this came the appreciation of, and need for a flexible interpretation of the Written Law, an interpretation which could be adapted and applied to the vagaries of changing circumstances. Out of this came the Pharisees whose goal was to return to the purity of following God's Written Law, thus preserving the Jewish community as God intended.

Most of us have learned to take a dim view of the Pharisees' traditions, so what has been said here might at least qualify the good intentions of the Oral Law. In fact, three main reasons are commonly cited to explain why writing the Oral Law down was prohibited for so long:

1. Writing down a code limits its scope and application to new situations; the principles must stay the same but the application should be fluid and adaptable.
2. The complexities of God's Laws as they interface with real life cannot be learned from textbooks; optimal understanding can only come through interaction with a live, master teacher[83].
3. If written down, Gentiles could eventually claim and twist as their own.

Eventually, due to fears of persecution and dispersion, these reasons for prohibition were overturned and the Talmud evolved.

But regarding the use of teachings already in circulation in Yeshua's day, the real point here is that although

---

83 which Yeshua was and is! See page 189.

185

the documents alluding to them were either written or compiled *after* the time of Yeshua, the oral traditions and interpretations they bare witness to reach back much further.

> The rabbinic sources make the claim that they are handing down old stories (known as Aggadah) and ancient Jewish (halachic) practices, **going back as far as the generation of Moses.**
>
> Therefore, when you see any rabbi citing an Aggadah or a halacha, ask yourself the question: did they just make this up themselves? The answer must be "Of course not." **Indeed, the Sages of that time period were called the "Tannaim" (repeaters), because their principle occupation was to pass on what they had learned, exactly as they had learned it. None of them would have even considered introducing something new to Judaism (G-d forbid, adding to the Torah). Anything they said was rooted in previous generations' words, and any rulings they made were founded upon the same principles that were already understood since Mount Sinai. (Letter from JewishEyes)**[84]

Notice that reproducing another sage's words was not considered *copying* but rather *repeating* since their comments shared a common source – the Torah; this is a subtle but extremely important distinction.

---

84 Jewish Eyes' staff in a personal letter to the author, Aug. 2016.

# THE (FIRST AND) LAST WORD

The focus of this book has been the importance of acknowledging the Jewishness of Messiah Yeshua and the treasures which we forfeit if we fail to appreciate this dimension. However, in highlighting one aspect of His total, immeasurable reality, it is easy to fall foul of "the law of unintended consequences." In concentrating on the Jewishness of Yeshua's words and various "hints" or connections with other Jewish teachers, we must keep in mind that, when all is said and done, **Yeshua was actually there in the beginning** and even before, as John declares: *"In the beginning was the Word, and the Word was with God, and the Word was God. He was with God in the beginning."*

Clearly, He knew in advance, all the sayings of all the teachers who were to come and in fact, shaped, foresaw and was wholly cognizant of the entire Jewish culture...along with every teaching that has ever been voiced or thought. Therefore, any theological resonance His words may have to other teachers is attributable to His timeless and omniscient divinity. He is like a man who threw a ball way ahead, only to leap forward to the exact time and place where he knew it would land. This is how He was able to both astound His audiences *and* connect through their culture.

Consequently, any allusions to Jewish ideas, stories or phrases — past, present or future — *were strictly for His audiences' benefit — theirs, not His*, as if needing to base, what were actually His and His Father's pre-existent teachings on any man's words. Actually, in all my research, I have found that **ALL** the words of Yeshua are original in their exact wording, not to mention those sayings and claims (such as the seven "*I Am's*") which simply must be utterly unique and true to Him and Him alone.

Yeshua, being God Himself made flesh, knows all things past, present, and future. He knows the end from the beginning and the beginning from the end (Isaiah 46:10). He knew the whole Oral Law inside and out before and after it was written. Any truth in other teachings [ultimately derives] only from He who **is**, the Way, **the TRUTH**, and the Life![85]

No sage could ever rival, not just the *truth* of His words, but also the *effect*. Yeshua tells us in Matthew 24 that, "*Heaven and earth will pass away, but my words will never pass away.*" Considering the immeasurable influence of the Bible and Yeshua's words in particular, on mankind over the last 2000 years, this is not hard to believe.

In contrast, the words of the Jewish sages have been consigned to virtual obscurity, requiring considerable effort to extract them from the annals of extra-biblical sources almost lost in the mists of time. This is unsurprising as, according to John 6, *His* words are **Spirit** (indestructibly eternal) and they are **Life** (indefatigably animated). No sage's words have ever consisted of such divine "substance."

---

85 Cheryl Zehr, director, Olive Press Publisher, in an email to the author, Feb. 17, 2017.

Like the air tanks which Captain Quint managed to attach to the shark in the movie "Jaws," Yeshua's words have a buoyancy which no monster, material or spiritual, can ultimately suppress. They have the power to leap off the page to break through oppressively Godless cultures and transform lives, leaving the sages' words — all due respect to them — as a comparative side show. "He is our living, Master Teacher, the Torah fulfilled, the Almighty Himself, interacting with us to teach us the Spirit, intent, and full application of Torah! His Sermon on the Mount was the beginning of that." [86]

Even though this book has been saying that if you deny the Jewishness of Yeshua, then you can not fully know Him, it is also true that when the sages and rabbis of the day heard Him speak, they marveled, were astounded and even silenced. It was said by their officers, *"Never has **anyone** spoken like this man"* (John 7:46 TLV). Notice that it was His *distinctiveness* from all other teachers which marked Him out — not His ability to quote lists of who said what, which, as has previously been said, was the Jewish sage thing to do. The following Scriptures make this clear:

**Regarding Yeshua's matchless *wisdom*...**

> *After three days they found him in the temple courts, **sitting among the teachers** [sages?], **listening to them and asking them questions**. Everyone who heard him was **amazed at his understanding and his answers**. ..."Why were you searching for me?" he asked. "Didn't you know I had to be in my **Father's house?**"But they did not understand what he was saying to them.*
> ~Luke 2: 46-49

---

86 Ibid.

*Coming to his hometown, he began **teaching the people in their synagogue, and they were amazed**. "Where did this man get this wisdom** and these miraculous powers?"*
~ Matthew 13:54

*"**All spoke well of him and were amazed at the gracious words** that came from his lips. "Isn't this Joseph's son?" they asked.* ~ Luke 4:22

*Not until halfway through the festival did Jesus go up to the temple courts and begin to teach. **The Jews there were amazed** and asked, "How did this man get such learning **without having been taught?**"* ~ John 7:14-16

*They were unable to trap him in what he had said there in public. And **astonished by his answer, they became silent**.* ~ Luke 20:26

*And no one dared to ask him any more questions.* ~ Luke 20:40

*No one could say a word in reply, and from that day on no one dared to ask him any more questions.* ~ Matthew 22:46

Most of us are familiar with Yeshua's encounter with Nicodemus. But have you noticed the minor but significant change that more recent translations have made? Take a look at John 3:10 from the KJV:

*"Art thou **a** master of Israel, and knowest not these things?"*

Now compare this with the NKJV:

*"Are you **the** teacher of Israel, and do not know these things?"*

The '*a*' (indefinite article) has become '*the*' (definite article) teacher of Israel. We might deduce from this that Nicodemus held an extremely high (or perhaps the highest) teaching position possible at that time. He was obviously a very important figure, either due to rank or reputation. Nicodemus hinted at his own elderly status ("*Can a man be born again when he is old*") but despite his considerable expertise and knowledge of other teachers' words, the originality and magnetism of *Yeshua's* words were clearly overwhelming! There must have been a very good reason for such a man to take such a risk in seeking to meet with Him!

**Regarding His Father being the singular *source of such wisdom...***

> *Jesus answered, "My teaching is not my own. It comes from the one who sent me."*
> ~ John 7:14-17

> *"I did not speak on my own, but **the Father who sent me commanded me to say all that I have spoken.** I know that his command leads to eternal life. So whatever I say is just what the Father has told me to say."* ~ John 12:49

> *"The words I say to you I do not speak on my own authority. Rather, it is the Father, living in me, who is doing his work."* ~ John 14:10

> *"I am telling you what I have seen in the Father's presence..."* ~ John 8:38

YESHUA is our Messiah, our Sar Shalom (Prince of Peace). He is our Savior and our Redeemer. He is our Wonderful Counselor and our Comforter. He is our Good Shepherd, our Adonai, our Healer, our

Great Physician. He is our Meleck haMlakhim and Adon haAdonim (King of kings and Lord of Lords). He is our Master and Rabbi. He is our Life and our LIGHT. He has the Name that is above every name to which every knee shall bow in Heaven and on earth and under the earth. He is eternal, having no beginning and no end. He is the firstborn of all creation. By Him and through Him and for Him all things were created. He is the head of all things and all things are under His feet. He is seated at the right hand of the Father. He and the Father are ONE.

He is the Ruler of the universe. He is the Vine. We can do nothing without abiding in Him, but with Him we can do all things that He calls us to do. He conquered the grave, overcame death, and annihilated Satan's power. He is our shield and our strong tower. We are safe in the shadow of His wings—His Tallit. He is our Heavenly Manna— the Bread of Life and our Living Water. He is our Passover Lamb, the very Lamb of God and our Yom Kippur scape goat. His eternally flowing, all powerful Blood is on Heaven's Mercy Seat washing away all our sin. HE IS OUR EVERYTHING—OUR VERY SALVATION.

YESHUA did not come to start a new religion. He is continuing the "religion" of the One (He Himself) who spoke the Torah from the fire, smoke, thunder, lightning, and long Shofar blast on Mt. Sinai; the One who parted the Red Sea and the Jordan; who felled the walls of Jericho; who raised children from the dead; who took Elijah to Heaven in chariots of fire; who defeated Sennacherib's army; and who caused King Cyrus to decree and fund the rebuilding of the Temple. He is the One who rides through the heavens to our help, majestic through the skies (Deut. 33:26); the Son of Man coming on the clouds of Heaven with power and great Glory.

It is HaShem's religion! The religion of the highest power and the greatest glory!! Yeshua came to explain that religion and renew and carry it forward through the greatest power of perfect, new-creation SALVATION, of complete forgiveness and total washing away of our sins, and total power to overcome both our sin and the enemy. He is our divine power to advance the Kingdom of Heaven and prevail against the gates of hell!!! It's not a new religion! It is the ancient religion straight from Heaven, straight from HaShem Himself fully revealed through His only begotten Son—HaShem embodied in flesh.[87]

---

87 Ibid. Can be found at http://olivepresspublisher.com/wp/wp-content/uploads/Who-is-Yeshua.pdf.

# BIBLIOGRAPHY

Asher, Rabbi Moshe ben, Ph.D. and Magidah Khulda bat Sarah, "The Yoke of the Kingdom of Heaven," *Khevra shel Kharakim*, 2007, gatherthepeople.org, <http://www. gatherthepeople.org/Downloads/KINGDOMS_YOKE.pdf> Accessed May 2017

Anderson, Lee Jr. "A Deeper Understanding of the Flood— Making the Most of the Message," *Answersingenesis.org*, April 1, 2014, <https://answersingenesis.org/the-flood/ making-the-most-of-the-message/>

*Babylonian Talmud (or Talmud Bavli)* contains the *Mishnah* (of which there is only one version) and the Babylonian Gamara (commentary on the *Mishnah* by various Rabbis who lived in Babylon). The *Mishnah* was finished c. 200 AD; the Babylonian Gemara was finished c. 500 AD.]

*Babylonian Talmud* Order: Nezikin (Damages), Tractate Maccot (Makkot): Chapter 2, Gemara of Mishna II.

Bialik, Haim Nachman, Jewish Poet, 1873-1934, a famous quote by him: "Reading the Scriptures in a translation (from Hebrew) is like kissing your bride through a handkerchief."

Bradford, Tom, "Old Testament Studies, Deuteronomy, Lesson 3, chapters 1 and 2," *TorahClass.com*, <http:// www.torahclass.com/teacher/38-old-testament-studies/old-testament-studies-deuteronomy/234-lesson-3-chapter-1-and-2 > Accessed May 2017.

Bullinger, E.W., *Number in Scripture: Its Supernatural Design and Spiritual Significance*, Eyre & Spottiswoode (Bible Warehouse) Ltd, 1921, Alacrity Press, 2014.

Chislett, Fr David SSC, "**Canon Jim Glennon** - Healing, the Kingdom of God, and Stress," *Streams of the River Making Glad the City of God Blog*, Feb. 8, 2014, http:// www.fministry.com/2014/02/canon-jim-glennon-healing-kingdom-of.html

*Cumming Study Guides,* "The Gilgamesh Epic," cummingsstudyguides.net, <https://www.cummingsstudyguides. net/Guides6/Gilgamesh.html> Accessed May 2017.

Eby, Preston, J., "Abraham's Bosom," *The Pathfinder,* Godfire.net, <https://www.godfire.net/eby/abrahams.html> Accessed May 2017.

Egan, Daniel, "The Gospel of John and a New Creation," *Bibletidbits.blogspot.com,* 1-29-2017, <http://bibletidbits. blogspot.com/2009/01/gospel-of-john-and-new-creation. html> Accessed May 2017.

Falk, Gerhard, PhD, "The Jewish Military Tradition: It Is Jewish to Fight!" *Jewish Buffalo on the Web,* jbuff.com, 3/22/01, <http://jbuff.com/c032201.htm> Accessed May 2017.

Franz, Gordon, "Let The Dead Bury Their Own Dead," *Archaeology and Biblical Research,* Article, 2009, <http:// www.biblearchaeology.org/post/2009/03/20/Let-the-Dead-Bury-Their-Own-Dead.aspx> Accessed May 2017.

Fruchtenbaum, Arnold G., *Footsteps of the Messiah: A Study of the Sequence of Prophetic Events,* Ariel Ministries, San Antonio, Texas, 1983, revised edition 2003. See the Table of Contents and some inside pages here: <https://www.logos. com/product/3899/the-footsteps-of-the-messiah-a-study-of-the-sequence-of-prophetic-events > Accessed May 2017.

_____, "The Place of the Dead," *Messianic Bible Study #107,* Ariel Ministries, San Antonio, Texas, ariel.org, <http:// www.arielm.org/dcs/pdf/mbs107m.pdf> Accessed May 2017.

_____, "The Three Messianic Miracles," *Messianic Bible Study #035,* Ariel Ministries, San Antonio, Texas, Apr. 2016, <http://www.messianicassociation.org/ezine48-af-three-messianic-miracles.htm> Accessed May 2017.

_____, *Yeshua, The Life of Messiah from a Messianic Perspective,* Vol. 1, 2, 3, Ariel Ministries, San Antonio, Texas, 2017

Gaechter, Paul, "Literary Art in the Gospel of Matthew." Katholisches Bibelwerk, 2013, <https://chiasmusresources.org/title> Accessed May 2017.

Gennon, Jim, Canon (See Chislett, Fr David)

Gordan, Nehemia, *The Hebrew Yeshua vs. the Greek Jesus,* Chapter 8 "Moses Seat," 3rd edition, Hilkiah Press, Atascosa, Texas, 2005

Hoshaiah (Osha'yah), *Bereshith (Genesis) Rabbah,* amora in Palestine. <http://www.jewishencyclopedia.com/articles/3056-bereshit-rabbah> Accessed May 2017.

_____, *Genesis Rabba,* Bereshith 4:6, online English translation at Archive.org/stream/RabbaGenesis, <https://archive.org/stream/RabbaGenesis/midrashrabbahgen027557mbp#page/n77/mode/2up> Accessed May 2017.

_____, *Genesis Rabba,* Vayera 48:8, online English translation at Archive.org/stream/RabbaGenesis, <https://archive.org/stream/RabbaGenesis/midrashrabbahgen027557mbp#page/n455/mode/2up> Accessed May 2017.

*Jerusalem Talmud* contains the *Mishnah* (of which there is only one version) and the Jerusalem Gamara (commentary on the *Mishnah* by various Rabbis who lived in Jerusalem and Isreal). The *Mishnah* was finished c. 200 AD; the Jerusalem Gemara was finished c. 400 AD.]

*Jerusalem Talmud,* Moed Qatan, c. 400 AD.

*JewishEncyclopedia.com,* "JOHANAN B. ZAKKAI,", <http://www.jewishencyclopedia.com/articles/8724-johanan-b-zakkai> Accessed May 2017.

*Jewishencyclopedia.com,* "Johanan-b-Zakkai", <http://www.jewishencyclopedia.com/articles/8724-johanan-b-zakkai> Accessed May 2017.

*Jewishencyclopedia.com,* <http://www.jewishencyclopedia. com/articles/3056-bereshit-rabbah> Accessed May 2017.

*Jewishvirtuallibrary.org,* <https://www.jewishvirtuallibrary. org/jsource/judaica/ejud_0002_0011_0_10216.html> Accessed May 2017.

Kalisher, Tzvi Hirsch, Rabbi: "The Finger of God-Torah Portion," *JewishJournal.com,* Accessed January 2017.

Lancaster, D. Thomas, Pastor, "New wine and old wineskins," Beth Immanuel Sabbath Fellowship, Hudson, Wisconsin, bethimmanuel.org, <http://www.bethimmanuel.org/ articles/new-wine-and-old-wineskins-parable-luke-536-39-re-examined> Accessed May 2017

Lebowitz, Rabbi Arych, Rabbi; "On the Daf: Bava Batra 126b," YUTorah.org <http://www.yutorah.org/daf.cfm/6025/ bava%20batra/126/b/> Accessed May 2017.

Lincoln, Andrew, "How Babies Were Made in Jesus' Time," *Biblical Archaeology Society,* Nov/Dec 2014.

McCane, Byron.R, "Let the Dead Bury Their Own Dead"; Secondary Burial and Matt 8:21–22," *Harvard Theological Review,* Volume 83, Issue 1, January 1990.

_____, *Roll Back The Stone: Death and Burial in the World of Jesus,* Trinity Press International, Harrisburg, Pennsylvania, 2003.

*Mishnah* (Hebrew: משנה "study by repetition") is the Oral Torah written down. (The Oral Torah is various rabbis' commentaries explaining how to live out—halakha—the Torah.) Finished c. 200 AD.

*Mishnah:* Perkei Avot (Ethics of the Fathers), <http://www. sefaria.org/Pirkei_Avot.5.15-18?lang=en&layout=lines&sid ebarLang=all> Accessed May 2017.

*Mishnah* order: Zera'im (Seeds), tractate: Berakhot (Blessings), <https://www.sefaria.org/Berakhot.61b?lang=bi> Accessed May 2017.

Neusner, Jacob and Neusner, M. M., editors, *The Book of Jewish Wisdom: The Talmud of the Well-Considered Life,* Global Publications, Binghamton University, Binghamton, NY, 2001.

*Sifre Deuteronomy,* Fourth century AD, English translation by Professor Marty Jaffee 2016, Stroum Center for Jewish Studies, University of Washington, JewishStudies. washington.edu, <http://jewishstudies.washington.edu/book/sifre-devarim/chapter/pisqa-357/> Accessed May 2017.

*Testament of Abraham,* Recension A, c. 50-100 AD, <http://www.earlyjewishwritings.com/testabraham.html> Accessed May 2017.

*The Jerusalem Talmud.* (See Jerusalem Talmud.)

Thomson, Rabbi Daniel, "Why Did Yeshua Use Spit to Heal?" *Jewish Eyes Newsletter,* Vol. XII-Issue XVII, Apr. 22-28, 2007, www.jewisheyes.org

_____, "Why did Jesus Walk on Water?" *Jewisheyes.org,* <http://www.jewisheyes.org/store/> Accessed May 2017.

*Wikipedia.org,* "First Council of Nicea" and "Separation of Easter computation from Jewish calendar," <https://en.wikipedia.org/wiki/First_Council_of_Nicaea#Overview > Accessed May 2017.

*Wikipedia.org,* "Sunday: Christian Usage," <https://en.wikipedia.org/wiki/Sunday#Christian_usage> Accessed May 2017.

# RECOMMENDED RESOURCES

Bradford, Tom, "Torah Class: Old/New Testament Studies," (audio download), torahclass.com

Fruchtenbaum, Arnold G., "Come and See" (Sequenced studies on essential theology from a Jewish roots perspective), *Ariel Ministries*, Ariel.org

Fruchtenbaum, Arnold G., *Footsteps of the Messiah: A Study of the Sequence of Prophetic Events*, Ariel Ministries, San Antonio, Texas, 1983, revised edition 2003.

Fruchtenbaum, Arnold G., "Systematic Theology," (mp3 download: 11 self-contained in-depth studies), *Ariel Ministries*, ariel.org

Fruchtenbaum, Arnold G., *Yeshua: The Life of Messiah from a Messianic Jewish Perspective*, Vol. 1, Ariel Ministries, San Antonio, Texas, 1983, April 2016.

Fruchtenbaum, Arnold G., *Yeshua: The Life of Messiah from a Messianic Jewish Perspective*, Vol. 2, Ariel Ministries, San Antonio, Texas, 1983, Jan. 2017.

Fruchtenbaum, Arnold G., *Yeshua: The Life of Messiah from a Messianic Jewish Perspective*, Vol. 3, Ariel Ministries, San Antonio, Texas, 1983.

Thomson, Rabbi Daniel, "Messianic Views of the Jewish Sages Series," (Weekly studies of the Torah, following the normal Jewish reading sequence which covers the entire Torah in one year; available free, under "Archive Learning"), JewishEyes.org.

Thomson, Rabbi Daniel, "Gospels and the Acts Through Jewish Eyes Series," (mp3 audio download), JewishEyes.org.

Thomson, Rabbi Daniel, "Jewish Roots of the Christian Faith Series" (Download), JewishEyes.org

# Acknowledgements

I would like to offer my thanks to those individuals and ministries who kindly, and freely, gave permission for me to refer to their insights and teaching. In a world where so often, it is the money that talks, they have exemplified the words of Yeshua – *"Freely you have received, freely give"*. Special thanks should be extended to the major contributors such as Dr Fruchtenbaum and the staff of Ariel Ministries; and Rabbi Daniel Thomson of *Jewisheyes* for his fascinating insights and gracious example of how the "Torah lifestyle" can be lived out in the "here and now."

It took 15 years of "sitting at the feet" of these Godly men until I felt I had arrived at a place where it was feasible to communicate some of these treasures to others who, like me, may be seeking a new direction in their study of God's Word. As a professional teacher, it has been my vocation to "reveal the concealed" and my prayer is that you, the reader, will have already begun to enjoy some of the anticipated benefits of studying The Word from a Jewish Perspective outlined in the preface.

Also, thanks to the publisher, Cheryl Zehr, the director of Olive Press Messianic and Christian Publisher. Annoyingly, your corrective interventions were hard to argue against and in hindsight, resulted in a much more balanced and refined final product. To Bertie, the springer spaniel whose persistent attentions would prise me from the laptop screen for some much needed head-clearing exercise. And finally, to my own "only begotten son," Darcy, whose continued interest – and nagging – urged me on to completion.

# Author Bio

Russ Constant was an architect's draughtsman for some years before attending St Luke's - Exeter University's School of Education in 1988 from where he graduated with a BA Honours degree in Education. He specialized in primary mathematics and since then has worked full time as a primary teacher in North Devon, England. Having benefited so much from the Messianic teachings of others, he wrote this book as a way of putting something back.

# Jewish Bread for Gentile Beggars!

is available at:

olivepresspublisher.com

amazon.com

barnesandnoble.com

and other online stores

## Store managers:

Order wholesale through:

Ingram Book Company

or by emailing:

olivepressbooks@gmail.com

www.ingramcontent.com/pod-product-compliance
Lightning Source LLC
Chambersburg PA
CBHW070350090426
42733CB00009B/1361